CW00550025

FOREST T

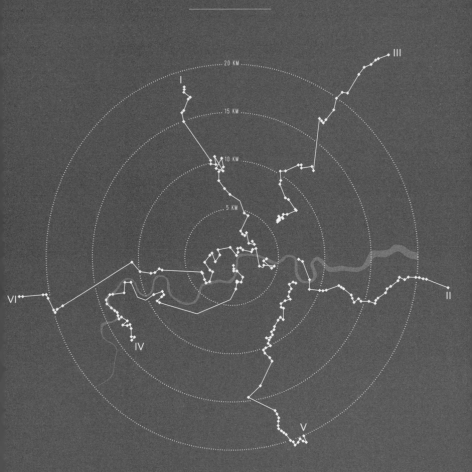

LONDON

IS

A

FOREST

LONDON

IS

A

FOREST

PAUL WOOD

Hardie Grant

QUADRILLE

Paul Wood is an artist, writer and an observer of urban nature with a lifelong passion for trees. He is the author of *London's Street Trees* and publishes a blog at thestreettree.com.
Follow him on social media @thestreettree.

To the Woods

PUBLISHING DIRECTOR Sarah Lavelle
COMMISSIONING EDITOR Zena Alkayat
EDITOR Nick Funnell
COVER DESIGN Claire Rochford
DESIGN & ILLUSTRATION Fieldwork Facility
PRODUCTION DIRECTOR Vincent Smith
PRODUCTION CONTROLLER Tom Moore

First published in 2019 by Quadrille,
an imprint of Hardie Grant Publishing

Quadrille
52–54 Southwark Street, London SE1 1UN
quadrille.com

Text © Paul Wood 2019
Design and layout © Quadrille Publishing Ltd 2019
Cover artwork © Pavel Bolotov / Adobe Stock

All rights reserved. No part of this publication may
be reproduced, stored in a retrieval system, or transmitted
in any form or by any means, electronic, electrostatic, magnetic
tape, mechanical, photocopying, recording, or otherwise,
without prior permission in writing from the publisher.

Cataloguing-In-Publication Data: A catalogue record
for this book is available from the British Library.

ISBN 978 1 78713 341 9

Printed in China

CONTENTS

A NOTE ON GPS

In the margins of the pages, dozens of GPS coordinates
have been added to help you locate landmarks and
individual trees, and allow you to loosely plot the trails,
either from your armchair or on foot.

FOREST TRAILS

HIGH BARNET
TO BARBICAN
PAGE 27 / 51.661776, -0.199169

ERITH TO
CANARY WHARF
PAGE 49 / 51.479218, 0.203076

EPPING TO
LONDON FIELDS
PAGE 73 / 51.693718, 0.113678

FOREST TRAILS

INTRODUCTION

London, according to one United Nations definition, is a forest. The city is home to over eight million trees, roughly one for every person, and enough for 20 per cent of the capital to be covered by tree canopy.

London may not immediately conform to everyone's idea of a forest, but this is an urban forest. Among the buildings, roads and railways, nature is thriving. This urban forest is a patchwork consisting of innumerable natural havens from the gardens of suburbia to ancient woodlands such as Coldfall and Lesnes Abbey Woods to parks and open spaces such as Wimbledon Common, Hyde Park and the tiny St Mary Aldermanbury Garden in the City. There is an incredible range of habitats, species and landscapes.

I admired views of the city from dozens of vantage points across London while researching this book. One of the finest, the remarkable panoramic view from Severndroog Castle, hidden in the woods of south east London, confirms that this city is exceptionally green. Looking out from the castle's battlements and over the tops of the trees, it's possible to see right across the city to Windsor in the far west, Wood Green and Highgate in the north and the North Downs to the south. From here, London's forest status is clear.

This book consists of six forest trails through London's green, and not-quite-so green spaces. They take in the trees as well as many of the other species encountered along the way. Today's forest has been shaped over many centuries, so I have also included insights and anecdotes about the history, heritage, ideas and people that have influenced it.

You'll also find GPS coordinates for dozens of landmarks and fascinating individual trees, allowing the trails to be plotted. I hope this book will hold as much appeal for intrepid explorers armed with phone, map and compass, as it will for those who prefer to discover the urban forest from the comfort of an armchair or a seat on the tube. Along the trails, I attempt to outline what the forest is and how it takes the form it does. I explore the rich diversity and interdependence of species through the fragile and entangled relationships between places, plants and animals, including us humans.

The urban forest's great diversity reflects that of the city itself. Like every aspect of London, it has been shaped by waves of human migration, global trade, exploration and conflict. As a result, new plants and animals have arrived – and escaped – from the city over the centuries. The forest is shaped by its geology, its architecture and its geography too. The primeval past can be glimpsed in the preserved tree stumps exposed at low-tide in the Thames mud at Erith, or in the ancient earthworks of Epping Forest. Not far from the city centre there are silent, secret woods and unkempt commons. There are heaths and downs alive with wildlife, and deer parks where old and sustainable management practices continue to be engaged in. All these precious survivors have witnessed the city grow around them and now they contribute to make it a green, interesting and healthy place to live and work. Elsewhere, new woods have grown up in the space of just a few decades, and everywhere, nature tirelessly does its best to reclaim the metropolis: along railway embankments, road verges, river banks and every patch of untended edgeland.

You may, like me, be surprised by the hundreds of fascinating veteran trees that can be found in all corners of the city. But surely the most surprising thing of all is that, against all the odds, swathes of London have survived in a state that is not too far distant from the original primeval wildwood.

The trails are not comprehensive, and the routes taken have been influenced as much by impulse and inquisitiveness as a desire to get from A to B. Various people's suggestions led me to specific places or individual trees that I had not seen before: Hutchinson's Bank at New Addington, or the baobab plane tree in Ravenscourt Park, for instance. I wanted to share my enthusiasm for some places and trees I knew already: the streets of Hackney, Kew Gardens or the Cheapside plane tree are a few of these. But many of the places I encountered, I knew little or nothing about before – Coldfall Wood, Hounslow Heath and the Charlton House mulberry tree were all exciting new discoveries. There are also dozens of places, trees and other life forms that do not get a mention: Hampstead Heath, Woodberry Wetlands, Brockwell Park are just a few. The ancient holm oak at Fulham Palace, the great surviving elms of Marylebone High Street or Ladywell Fields and the veteran Tottenham oak will have to content themselves with a passing mention here, as will London's declining hedgehog population, its increasing number of wood pigeons and the various rodents with which we share the city.

If this book can offer some new insights into London's truly remarkable urban forest, raise awareness about urban nature, or inspire you to experience some of the places I mention for yourself, then I will feel the forest's future is more secure.

KEY TERMS

The following terms are used frequently throughout the book and are expanded on here for reference.

Forest
'Forest' is a complex term with many meanings. It's generally taken to be a large area covered by trees. But there are also large tracts of treeless moors in Scotland called forests, and London, with a mere 20 per cent tree coverage, is considered one, too. In England the word and concept originated with the Normans, who used it to describe land set aside as the king's hunting grounds, which usually had a high density of trees. In order to enable a sustainable supply of game within a forest, special forest laws were put in place to manage the land. These stipulated who could do what, covering such activities as the grazing of livestock and wood cutting. Each forest would have its own set of complex laws and a bureaucracy to uphold them. Epping Forest is a good example of a large forest with ancient roots and, while no longer managed for royal hunts, it is still governed by a long list of bye-laws imposed by its current owner, the City of London Corporation.

Perhaps London is better understood as an urban forest, a term used frequently in this book as shorthand to mean all trees and green open spaces in the city. This includes patches of woodland, parks, railway embankments, land around estates, the gardens of private homes and street trees. The urban forest is critical for ensuring the city is 'liveable', meaning that it is both a pleasant place to live and work.

Ancient woodland

Woodlands that have existed since before 1600 are classed as ancient. Few woods were planted at that time, so woodland areas that remain from then could in many cases be much older, even dating back to the original primeval forest that once covered much of London. Ancient woodlands have distinctive flora and fauna communities as well as unique soils that have built up over centuries or millennia. In the past all the capital's areas of ancient woodland would have been managed using sustainable techniques handed down over many generations. A wood's claim to ancient status is supported by historical documentary evidence as well as the presence of – often rare – plants known as 'indicator species'. These include wild service tree, woodland (or midland) hawthorn, herb paris, wood anemone and bluebell. Examples of ancient woodlands in London are Oxleas, Highgate, Selsdon and Coldfall Woods.

Veteran and ancient trees

Old trees may be classified as veteran or ancient, but there is a subtle difference between the two definitions. Veteran trees are those that look old and often show characteristics of old age such as hollow trunks, great height or enormous girths. It is a subjective categorisation given to great, often venerable trees that are admired and valued. Ancient trees, on the other hand, are those that have been verified as very old, usually through documentary evidence such as old maps, prints or written accounts. Ancient and veteran status varies between species. A 150-year-old plane tree is not ancient, but could be veteran, while a birch tree of the same age could be afforded both veteran and ancient status as the species rarely survives past 100. Examples of ancient trees in London are the Royal Oak in Richmond Park and the Totteridge Yew. Veteran trees might include many of the sweet chestnuts in Greenwich Park or the large planes in Berkeley Square. All you need to remember is that all ancient trees are veterans, but not all veterans are ancient. The Woodland Trust maintains a database of ancient and veteran trees at ati.woodlandtrust.org.uk and the Ancient Tree Forum does important work recording and raising awareness of them.

The Great Trees of London
The Great Trees of London is a list of 61 notable trees in the capital that was originally drawn up after the Great Storm of 1987, which caused the destruction of thousands of trees across the city. It was initiated by the charity Trees for Cities, which compiled a list of 41 trees nominated by the public. Twenty more entries were added in 2008. Since then, several of the trees on the list have disappeared, while many notable trees perhaps worthy of inclusion remain waiting in the wings.

Timber and wood
When London's ancient woodlands were managed in the past, they produced a great deal of wood and relatively little timber. Timber is the product of single felled trees: large planks and beams typically used in the construction of buildings and ships. The hammerbeam roof at Westminster Hall or the ships built at Deptford would require large quantities of timber, but very little of it would have been locally sourced. Instead, London's woodlands were managed to produce wood, a renewable crop derived from the new growth of coppice stools or pollard boles and normally harvested every ten to 20 years. Most wood produced in the likes of Highgate or Lesnes Abbey Woods was used for firewood, but some would also have been employed to make smaller items such as tool handles, chopping boards, vessels and shoe lasts. Highly skilled woodsmen – the people who worked the woodlands – would also have made hurdles, fencing, charcoal and other products at sites in Epping Forest, the Great North Wood and elsewhere.

Coppicing, pollarding and wood pasture
The pockets of ancient woodland that still exist in London have been managed sustainably for many, many generations, and are now legally protected. In the past they were looked after as vital sources of wood and timber, and nowadays we continue to manage our woodlands for recreation, conservation and ecological reasons. Woodland management practices include coppicing, pollarding and wood pasture. Coppicing is the technique of cutting trees back to a 'stool' that's level with the woodland floor from where multiple branches then re-emerge to be harvested every eight to 20 years. Pollarding is similar, but involves cutting back the trees

to a single trunk, or 'boling' that allows branches to regrow out of reach of deer or other animals that would feed on the young shoots. Pollards are typically found in areas given over to wood pasture in the past. This is the practice of growing trees more or less densely among land used to graze animals. The effects of coppicing can be seen in Lesnes Abbey, Coldfall, Highgate and Queen's Woods, while pollarding was carried out in Epping Forest and Richmond Park. Richmond Park is also a good example of a wood pasture landscape – kept in check by the deer. Formerly, places such as Barnes Common and Bostall Heath would have been managed as wood pasture. Street and park trees continue to be managed through pollarding, though nowadays the intention is to maintain size and shape rather than produce a regular crop of firewood.

Deer park
Essentially, a deer park is enclosed land on which deer are kept. Several open spaces in London have been deer parks in the past, including Hyde Park and Kensington Gardens, Greenwich Park, and Chingford Plain. Richmond Park and Bushy Park are examples of surviving deer parks and illustrate their unique characteristics. Most deer parks were created (or imparked) in the Middle Ages, though Richmond Park is unusual in the fact that it was imparked more recently, in the seventeenth century. The specific historic practice of imparking describes how land – often common land – was enclosed by high fencing or walls to keep the deer in and, generally speaking, commoners and their livestock out. Deer parks are often composed of large areas of open grass or heath dotted with individual trees with smaller patches of woodland. They are frequently rich in veteran and ancient trees together with rare grassland and heathland habitats. Because of their age, deer parks are likely to host rare flora and fauna, including insects and fungi associated with very old trees. Their deer inhabitants (mostly fallow and red deer) live in semi-wild, but protected conditions and historically would have been hunted by the monarch and their elite circle. All deer were the property of the crown and venison was regarded as a royal food, so deer and deer parks were exclusively in the gift of the monarch to bestow on favoured nobles. Deer parks are different from royal hunting forests by the fact that they are enclosed and typically have a greater concentration of deer.

Common land and enclosure
Commons such as Clapham, Wandsworth or Barnes would once
have been used by local people to exercise their common rights to
graze livestock, collect firewood or grow food and so on. Common
land was owned by the crown, aristocratic estates, the church or
other institutions, but people who lived nearby, often parishioners or
tenants, had rights to use it. However, between the seventeenth and
nineteenth centuries, landlords started to enclose large swathes of
common land by either purchasing the common rights or exploiting an
Act of Parliament that allowed them to evict commoners. This highly
controversial practice resulted in social upheaval and a dramatic change
in land use that saw small peasant farms give way to more modern
industrialised forms of agriculture. These changes also coincided with
the industrial revolution and the large-scale movement of people from
the countryside to expanding towns and cities. Today many commons
still exist in London, although most, such as Clapham or Wandsworth,
have now become parks maintained by local authorities. However, a few
– Wimbledon and Barnes Commons, for instance – retain the appearance
and ecology of traditional common land.

Secondary woodland
Secondary woodland consists of trees that have grown up naturally
on land that has not always been wooded. Much urban woodland can
be categorised as secondary. When a piece of terrain is left to its own
devices, nature starts to recolonise and within 20 years or so it will be
dominated by trees and feel like a young woodland. Although ancient
woods can be secondary, these must have emerged prior to 1600 and,
on the whole, most of London's secondary woodland is much younger.
Secondary woods may include species – such as sycamore, Turkey oak
or horse chestnut – that have seeded themselves but are rarely found
in ancient woodland. There is often a great deal of ivy, too. Wick
Woodland, Bramley Bank, Gunnersbury Triangle and Nunhead
Cemetery are all secondary woodlands.

Downland

Chalk downland is grassland that overlays the chalk hills of southern
Britain. The North Downs of Kent and Surrey are situated at the extreme
southern edge of London, with a few areas, such as Hutchinson's Bank
in Croydon, just crossing over into the city boundaries. Chalk is very
porous and the soils overlaying it are thin, poor and unable to retain
as much moisture as heavier clay. Downland has a distinctive alkaline,
or calcareous, character reflecting the underlying chalk and, as a result,
supports specific lime-tolerant plant species. Because the soils are so
poor (or unimproved) they weren't favoured for growing crops and
so downland has survived as an ancient, semi-natural grassland habitat
maintained over millennia of animal grazing. Downland is particularly
associated with rare orchid species and other flowering plants such as
milkwort, viper's bugloss, horseshoe vetch and salad burnet. It also
supports a specific invertebrate community rich in butterflies, including
blues and skippers. If downland was left ungrazed, like any other land,
it would soon return to scrub and within just a few decades, secondary
woods would grow up.

Lowland heath

Like downland, heathland is open, unimproved land kept in check
by grazing animals. However, it has a quite different character because
the underlying soils are acid sands, gravels and clays that give rise to
a different plant community. In London, small pockets of acid lowland
heath survive in places such as Lesnes Abbey Woods, Addington Hills
and Hounslow Heath where shrubby plants such as heather, bracken and
gorse dominate. Lowland heaths support large and diverse invertebrate
communities, including many types of dragonfly. They are also noted
for their bird and reptile communities.

Native and non-native species

Officially, plants and animals can be called 'native' to Britain if there is
evidence that they lived here before the British Isles were cut off from
the European continent. This separation is thought to have occurred
about 8,000 to 9,000 years ago at the end of the last ice age when
melting glaciers raised sea levels and caused the flooding of the land
bridge that connected southern Britain with the continental mainland.

In theory, once Britain became an island, its flora and fauna were thought to have been 'fixed'. Thus anything arriving after that time must have been introduced and is classed as 'non-native' or sometimes 'alien'. But these definitions seem problematic. First, they deny the possibility that certain now-familiar plants or animals might have arrived under their own steam. Who's to say, for instance, that seeds never hitched a ride with migrating geese, or that severed tree boughs loaded with ripe fruit never floated across the Channel? It also discounts the useful plants and animals that human carriers such as Neolithic farmers, Roman armies and Anglo-Saxon, Viking or Norman settlers brought here in the past. In short, they are terms that seem to reflect political geography rather than ecological realities. As such, they allow a species such as sycamore to be tagged a 'non-native' weed despite occurring naturally in northern France and Belgium – areas far closer to much of the UK than, say, the 'native' Scots pine, which only exists naturally well north of Glasgow.

Invasive species
Some non-native or, to use a less loaded term, recently arrived species have become invasive. This means that they thrive so well on some sites that they can alter their character and tip the ecological balance away from longer established but less fecund plants. Sometimes they can even form monocultures where little else can flourish. Because invasive species have not evolved side-by-side with the plants and animals they encounter here, they can wreak havoc. Four are regarded as particularly problematic: Japanese knotweed, common rhododendron, giant hogweed and Himalayan balsam. Evergreen rhododendron, for instance, can quickly dominate the understory of woodlands, such as those in Richmond Park, shading out bluebells and other plants that make up the finely balanced ground flora. This can also affect the regeneration of tree seedlings, starving them of light and leaving them unable to survive in the dense, dark conditions they create. Invasive species tend to have no, or very few, natural enemies to keep them in check and support few creatures with food or shelter. Tree of heaven, buddleia and some varieties of eucalyptus are also on the watchlist for showing signs of potential invasiveness.

Pollen record

The pollen record refers to identifiable grains of plant pollen preserved in rocks and soils. Pollen conserved in peat, for example, can be dated and has helped determine which plants may be classified as native or non-native based on their presence at the time of the British Isles' separation from continental Europe at the end of the last ice age. Pollen records can also tell us about the relative abundance of a plant at points in the past. For instance, they show that small-leaved lime was very common over much of south-east England but started to decline about 4,000 years ago. At that time it would have been the dominant tree in Epping Forest, but it is now virtually absent. Scholars continue to investigate why this might be the case.

Classification

This book generally uses common names for plants and animals. Where used, scientific names have been italicised. An example of a common name is London plane; its scientific name is *Platanus* × *hispanica*.

Cultivar

A cultivar is a named variety of a plant with specific characteristics that are distinct from the regular species. A copper beech, for instance, is a cultivar of the familiar beech tree. It differs from the green-leaved species by having purple leaves, a mutation that may have been selected from nature, or selectively bred by horticulturists. In order to retain the specific genes that produce its distinct features, a cultivar must be reproduced clonally. Clonal reproduction is carried out by methods such as root suckering, grafting or taking cuttings. Because cultivars are genetically identical, any less desirable features are also retained alongside the more desirable ones. Common cultivars include the Irish yew, familiar apple and garden rose varieties and the 'Chanticleer' pear, a distinct cultivar of the callery pear with a regular, conical habit and a frequent street tree throughout London. To classify cultivars, botanists append their specific name to the scientific name, in this case *Pyrus calleryana* 'Chanticleer'.

Green belt

London's green belt was established after the Second World War and now covers half a million hectares of land encircling the city where development is restricted. Its intention was to stop urban sprawl and provide London with defined edges beyond which building would not be allowed. But while it has been effective in stopping the geographical growth of the city, it is not without its critics. Some partly attribute the inflated cost of housing in London to the restrictions on development in the green belt. Others suggest that conditions are now very different from the ones that characterised postwar London and the extent and purpose of the green belt should now be reviewed. However, politicians seem afraid to tackle these issues and so the status quo of the 1950s remains in place. At the same time, the green belt itself has seen many changes. Areas that were once farmland or land managed in traditional ways beneficial to wildlife have in many places been swallowed up by golf courses, health spas and other developments.

Edgeland

In this book, the term edgeland is used to describe parcels of land where nature has been given a relatively free rein. These include spaces such as railway embankments and roadsides, river and canal banks, and the small strips of land found on the fringes of car parks, between offices and next to industrial buildings. Marion Shoard first coined the term in her essay 'Edgelands of Promise' in 2000. Her interpretation is broader and considers a multi-faceted landscape that exists where city and countryside merge: 'the edgelands – that is, the hotchpotch collection of superstores, sewage works, golf courses and surprisingly wildlife-rich roughlands which sit between town and country in the urban fringe.'

Ecosystem services

In London, the urban forest provides a number of beneficial 'ecosystem services' for Londoners, many of which are quantifiable. These include:
– *Carbon storage* Trees absorb and store carbon while increasing oxygen in the atmosphere through photosynthesis.

– *Climate moderation* Reduced temperatures in the vicinity of
shade-giving trees can in turn reduce humans' energy use for
air conditioning.
– *Absorption of airborne pollutants* Trees can absorb some airborne
pollution particles and many gaseous particles through their leaves.
Absorbed pollutants may be stored in the tree's plant matter.
– *Reduction of flash flooding risk* Trees soak up rainfall and can help
to capture storm water.

In addition, there's increasing evidence to show that access to urban
green spaces and living near large numbers of trees can benefit people's
mental and physical health. It's also no doubt true that the proximity
of trees in a neighbourhood can positively influence house values.
Lastly, we shouldn't forget the valuable and hugely important ecosystem
service provided by pollinating insects, which rely on trees and other
plants for food and shelter.

CAVAT

The Capital Asset Value for Amenity Trees (CAVAT) is a system
devised by London's tree officers in order to provide a monetary value
for urban trees. CAVAT uses three key measures. The initial valuation
is based on girth – the diameter of the trunk measured at breast height
(or DBH). The bigger the girth, the more valuable the tree. This value
is then adjusted according to an estimate of how much longer a tree
might live. If it's five years or less, the tree's value will plummet to
0 per cent. But if it's 80 years or more, it will remain at 100 per cent.
The population density of the area surrounding the tree is the third
measure. If it is more than 119 people per square hectare – as is the case
in some London boroughs – the valuation will increase by 250 per cent.
However, the CAVAT system does not take into account the variations
in age and size that different species might eventually reach, nor their
relative rarity.

Natural and semi-natural habitats

Truly natural habitats that have not been subject to human influence
do not exist in London, but semi-natural habitats shaped by sustainable
human intervention do. These include ancient woodlands, heathlands
and downlands. Spared from herbicides or fertilisers or significant

landscaping, their soils have remained undisturbed, allowing plant communities to evolve over centuries. They will also have been managed in similar, traditional ways for generations through practices such as grazing, coppicing or pollarding. As a result they will support the rich animal and plant communities associated with these habitats. These semi-natural ancient landscapes offer an echo of the past character of the city. But it would be foolish to think they represented an ideal or 'original' landscape unaffected by the past and continuing impact of climate, evolution and human intervention.

HIGH
BARNET
TO
BARBICAN

THE MONKEN HADLEY OAK

On the high ground at the very edge of London, not far from where
Hertfordshire begins, is the leafy urban village of Monken Hadley.
There, by the side of the main road, an impressive old English oak tree
stands, towering above all around it. It's perhaps 30 metres high with
a broad, rounded crown, and appears to be a maiden, an oak that has
not been pollarded, or lopped. It must be 200 years old, middle-aged,
and is in rude health: it could easily see out another two centuries
shading the highway and marking the way. The road it stands by – now
the not-so-grand A1000 – was an important medieval route between
the cathedral city of St Albans and London. At Monken Hadley, then
in rural Hertfordshire, and still 11 gruelling miles from the Thames,
the road cut through extensive woods known as the Southaw before
emerging at the market town of Chipping Barnet, better known these
days as High Barnet.

    The Monken Hadley Oak may once have been a boundary
or marker tree, perhaps the second or third generation oak to inhabit
the spot. One of its predecessors could have been preserved from the
Southaw after it was stripped back for other land uses. As London's
population grew, food and fuel were the most in-demand resources,
and the woods may first have been used to produce firewood, then
turned into farmland to feed the urban masses. It would only have been
in the last 100 to 150 years that London's other great need, living space,
would have impinged on land use in these northern edges and, by that
time, the Southaw would have been long gone.

51.661776, -0.199169

Boundary trees, though, can still be found around the city. Their original purposes may now be forgotten, but they're still able to remind us of a time when natural landmarks were important demarcations of borders between landowners, parishes, rights of way and other jurisdictions. Of course, boundary trees don't stop being boundary trees just because their original purpose is now less important; often the thresholds they mark are still in use. These days it's us who, in our networked, GPS-determined wanderings, have little need for physical markers. Maybe this oak once demarcated a more significant border than the rather workaday division it now determines between a front garden and Hadley Green, but its sheer physical presence still focuses our attention.

Although the biggest tree in the vicinity, the oak competes in age with a smaller, more unusual survivor just down the road: a <u>small-leaved lime</u>, perhaps another tree planted or preserved to mark a boundary. Now rarely seen in natural, or semi-natural habitats, small-leaved limes were once common constituents of woods throughout southern England. Today their presence is believed to indicate the site of ancient woodland – woods that can be traced back more than 400 years, of which there are a surprising number in London. Small-leaved limes should not be confused with hybrid common limes – the much more frequent lime tree of suburbia that in summer produces honeydew, the scourge of garage-less car owners – though they are some of their parents. This veteran small-leaved lime might suggest that the Southaw survived, at least in part, until well after the medieval period and that it may have been a mixed wood containing oak and lime.

While no longer densely wooded, these northern borderlands are certainly leafy and have preserved a patchwork of green spaces, remarkable individual trees, wooded dells and – not to be underestimated – lots of large gardens. Rather than ending abruptly with a single line of back-garden fences encircling the city, London thus blends subtly and porously into the green belt, that useful but perennially threatened girdle of countryside that acts partly as London's great lungs and guarantor of the city's limits.

51.664133, -0.199175

CHIPPING BARNET

The marker trees and outermost fringes of London quickly give way to the start of the conurbation proper at High Barnet. The end of one branch of the Northern Line, this is most definitely London, its credentials immortalised in Cockney rhyming slang's appropriation of the Barnet Fair. The name High Barnet refers to the town's elevated position on a ridge above the Dollis Valley. Join the nearby London Loop – a signposted footpath circumnavigating the city – at King George's Fields and a sweeping view opens up to the towers of Stratford and Canary Wharf, and the high ground beyond where the dense remnants of Oxleas and Lesnes Abbey Woods nestle. You'll find London plane trees here, too, as if to further underscore where you are. Fine Georgian houses somewhere between country manors and townhouses overlook Hadley Green where large copper beeches, poplars and pines vie with oaks to complete the canopy. And, tantalisingly, a mature cedar of Lebanon rises behind a high old brick wall.

51.659122, -0.199792

The most distinctive and perhaps the loveliest of cedars, the flattened, horizontally branched cedar of Lebanon is a species under threat. After millennia of logging, it is now restricted to a fraction of its former natural range in the mountains of the Middle East. The last pure stands are now protected on Mount Lebanon, while in Turkey, serious efforts are being made to replant large tracts of cedar forest. The tree is so iconic to the Lebanese that its handsome silhouette is emblazoned on their national flag.

The cedar of Lebanon has been known for centuries in London. The great tree lover, gardener and Deptford resident, John Evelyn, mentions it in his 1664 treatise '*Sylva*' and Georgian London was the scene of a cedar-planting fad. Eighteenth- and early nineteenth-century landscape designers were much taken by the cedar's striking cones and mature silhouette, planting them in parks and gardens wherever space allowed. We should regard this craze as a gift for today's modern Londoners: cedars of Lebanon take at least a century to attain the size and shape that the Georgians admired. Large and spreading, these enigmatic trees also require that premium London commodity – growing space – meaning that not only are they predominantly restricted to the more spacious outer boroughs, but that they are rarely planted for future generations to enjoy these days.

Following the London Loop, there's another boundary tree that marks the path's emergence from King George's Fields, this time a multi-stemmed hornbeam. The hornbeam, along with oak, is the tree most synonymous with London. The city lies in the middle of the hornbeam belt – an arc sweeping from Essex and Kent through Hertfordshire and Buckinghamshire and out to Berkshire. All the tracts of ancient woodland in London support the species, and there are large specimens throughout the city.

Constructed of brick and concrete liberally interspersed with Tudorbethan half timbering, these suburban metrolands mark one of the front lines of urban forest destruction. Elsewhere in the city, residents concerned with the effects of pollution and global warming appear to support the well-documented benefits of trees and tree-planting local authorities and residents groups act upon them. But here in these interwar developments, perhaps because of their distance from the crowded centre and their less densely packed amenities, trees are cast out and the car is king. Many front gardens have been concreted over and the small, private plots of greenery that, en masse, once made up a significant natural estate filled with plants and the wildlife they supported have virtually disappeared. Not so long ago almost every garden held the possibility of some horticultural bounty, provoking envy and fascination in curious passers-by. But now suburban staples such as clipped privet hedges, fragrant roses and bountiful fruit trees have become distant memories in these parts. Walk down a typical street such as Meadway in Barnet and you get a fair idea – only one in ten front gardens has any plants to speak of, and even fewer have trees. Beyond the concrete forecourts and extensions, you can glimpse leafy canopies in the private realms of back gardens, but, on these forest front lines, roadside trees are too few and far between to have much impact. How would the shiny Fords and Nissans get into their off-road berths with street trees blocking the driveway?

These semi-detached Metroland developments were constructed in the 1920s and '30s for aspiring middle-class communities to coalesce around railway stations. Office workers could easily commute into the metropolis and come home to family-friendly country living on the city fringes in the evenings. Perhaps in the future, convenient and cheap driverless vehicles might reduce the need for privately owned cars that stay parked up 90 per cent of the time and front gardens could once again become part of the urban forest. Replacing a brand-new Mercedes with a characterful mulberry would add so much to the streetscape, while a renewed enthusiasm to tend front gardens might deepen the sense of community.

DOLLIS BROOK TO TOTTERIDGE

Below Barnet, the Dollis Brook meanders through a broad green tract that effectively pauses the city's northern expansion. Unlike most natural London waterways, this small stream has resisted culverting for its entire length, running from Totteridge Fields near the A1 and forming a looping arc that merges with the Mutton Brook to become the River Brent near the North Circular at Brent Cross. It's hidden among trees that include white willows, so-called because their leaves take on a silvery hue caused by fine white hairs on the undersides of the leaves. Willows are also associated with water and here they define the course of the brook. From the wet woodland and fields around the stream, a path leads through dense scrub. Here, shrubs that might be seen in field hedges have been left to grow, entirely enveloping the path with blackthorn, hawthorn, guelder rose and field maple. Just a few hundred metres from the Northern Line, this route feels distinctly un-urban. The surrounding species are familiar to any country rambler and the dense vegetation cuts out the city: there are no aircraft noises overhead, and no glimpses of buildings or people through the impenetrable bush. Only the asphalt, street lights and a burnt-out moped dumped in the undergrowth act to remind you that you're still in London. But it's certainly not a well-trodden path, and it would be a brave soul who took it after dark. After many turns, the path eventually emerges in another sought-after locale: the former village of Totteridge, now an enclave of multi-million-pound houses hidden beneath trees and behind high fences.

Totteridge is the location of an ancient yew – London's oldest tree – which, in common with other veteran yews, is to be found in a churchyard. St Andrew's Church was constructed in the eighteenth

51.642031, -0.200185

51.640380, -0.202900

51.632383, -0.200550

century, already many centuries after its ancient resident had first emerged into the sunlight. Some accounts put the tree at a staggering 2,000 years old, though more conservative estimates say it is between 1,000 and 2,000 years. Either way, it's an astonishing survivor. Even if it is just 1,000 years old, it would have been a sapling at the time of the Norman conquest. If it's 2,000 years old, it would have been in situ before the Romans arrived.

As these estimates suggest, dating ancient trees is an imprecise science. By their nature, very old trees are in decline and may well have been for centuries. As with humans, tree ageing is marked by a gradual falling apart while trying to hold things together. Often the heartwood – the middle of the trunk – will have died, leaving hollows, and large branches may have succumbed to gravity centuries before. It's not uncommon to find younger yew trees larger than this particular example – some churchyards sport magnificent specimens perhaps only 200 or so years old. Indeed, St Andrew's has another yew that at first glance could be mistaken for our ancient tree. It's an Irish, or Florence Court yew, a type much planted in the nineteenth century and only 'discovered' in 1767, making it at least 800 years younger than its neighbour.

Irish yews are a cultivar of regular yews, which is to say a distinct, named form or strain of the species, differentiated by their fastigiate, upward-sweeping branches. They maintain a neat, strong evergreen silhouette and are frequently encountered in London's burial grounds. But the most interesting thing about Irish yews is the story of how they were discovered and their subsequent introduction to the urban forest. Back in 1767, a farmer in County Fermanagh found a couple of unusual yew seedlings growing on a mountainside. He dug them up and planted them on, giving one to his landlord, the wonderfully named Lord Mount Florence. This aristocratic seedling was planted in the grounds of his lordship's stately home, Florence Court, where it thrives to this day and is the original Irish yew of which every specimen around the world – now numbering in their millions – is a scion. The seeds of Irish yews do not produce other Irish yews, instead they revert to the regular species, so every tree starts life as a cutting from another Irish yew and is identical to that original tree. The Florence Court tree alone has had 20,000 cuttings taken from it by enthusiastic propagators.

While not all of London's trees can claim to have been found on an Irish mountain, many familiar plants can tell similar stories involving the discovery of a striking individual specimen in the wild or in a plant nursery, and the maintenance of its singular characteristics by reproducing it through grafts or cuttings. The downside of this practice is that every tree is a clone – genetically identical to every other tree of the same cultivar – which means any weaknesses or problems with the original plant are also carried forward with its more admirable features. Apple varieties are also all produced in this same way: Pink Lady or James Grieve, for instance, come from genetically identical trees. Try to grow one of the pips, and the result will be unpredictable – you're likely to produce a completely different, and most likely inferior, crab apple tree. It's the same for roses, dahlias and tulips, as well as copper beeches and weeping willows. Lots of plants in this urban forest are clones of special plants that either appeared quite naturally, like the Irish yew, or have been intensely bred over decades or centuries, such as hybrid tea roses.

COLDFALL WOOD

Beyond Totteridge, London becomes more densely patchworked. The city forest takes on a decidedly more urban feel, with gardens, parks and the edgelands of railway lines making up the bulk of its green areas. Things are tighter now, boundaries are more pronounced, and the canopy becomes more managed. But there are still plenty of open spaces, and as you get closer to the city centre, ironically perhaps, some of London's precious ancient woodland remnants start to reveal themselves, providing a glimpse into the past and, maybe, a model for the future.

Where the boroughs of Barnet and Haringey abut, one of these ancient survivors clings on. Up until less than a century ago, Coldfall Wood was much larger than its current 14 hectares. An 1873 Ordnance Survey map of Middlesex shows a patchwork of woodlands, farmland and villages, and at this time, Coldfall's southern boundary was Fortis Green and its eastern boundary was almost at Tetherdown, both of which are now merely the enigmatic names of Muswell Hill streets. Coldfall is another obscure name, thought to derive from 'coal', a reference to its historic use as a renewable source of firewood, and

51.596626, -0.159285

'fall', an ancient name for a coppiced woodland. Bought by the council in 1930 to ensure its borders did not shrink any further, the wood now bears little sign of its working past. Step beneath its cool, dark canopy and the outside world becomes almost immediately more distant as the dense vegetation dramatically reduces visibility and perceptions close in. As your eyes adjust to the gloom, short jerky rustlings on the barren floor reveal themselves to be robins or wrens. Ears, too, have to get used to a more closed environment: traffic becomes little more than a low hum and unseen dogs bark not far away. Those robins and wrens startle by singing loudly close by as jays silently patrol higher branches and grey squirrels scurry all around.

Once accustomed to the dramatic difference between the outside world and the interior of Coldfall Wood, you can start apprehending this remarkable oasis. Bizarrely, there are asphalt pavements, street lights and bins, presumably to encourage 'sticking to the path'. But it is easy to diverge into the relative wilderness. The wood consists of large oak trees – both pedunculate, or English, and sessile are here – and hornbeam, plus a few others, including two ancient woodland 'indicator' species, wild service and midland hawthorn. Traditionally, Coldfall was managed as 'coppice with standards', a practice whereby large, straight-trunked, or 'standard' trees, usually oaks, were left to mature above a dense understory of coppice. Coppicing is the practice of regularly cutting trees back to the ground, every 20 years or so, and allowing the regeneration of multiple stems from the resulting stool. It's a sustainable management technique that's still practised on a small scale, mostly for ecological reasons, and was a way to produce a regular crop of wood. In Coldfall, as in London's other ancient woods, hornbeam was the most frequent crop, valued as high-quality firewood and for a range of artisanal uses such as making tool handles, shoe lasts and chopping boards. Save for a few small pockets of recent coppicing, Coldfall's coppice appears to have last been harvested around 90 years ago and since then the hornbeams have been left to grow. Managed in this way, the wood's ancient coppice stools may be centuries old. Now, though, each one accounts for just one, two or maybe three large trees that have attained such heights that they mingle with the oaks to form a dense, dark and sometimes eerie place. These ageing hornbeams appear to have struggled to reach the canopy, creating wiry, athletic trunks that you can admire at the same time as you marvel at the wood's quiet determination to be deep forest in the city.

As we humans have evolved from wanting to tame the forest to wanting to preserve and live with it, it is now inconceivable that this much-loved urban wood could be anything other than that: an ancient wood. But only a hundred years ago, a different attitude prevailed – one mirroring how wildernesses have been subdued the world over. By 1913 Creighton Avenue had bisected the wood and by 1931 a series of new suburban streets to the south had been laid out, including the respectable and storied-sounding turnings of Beech Drive and Church Vale. The Second World War paused development, but by the early 1950s the destruction of the lower reaches of a respectably sized woodland – its extent perhaps unchanged for centuries – was complete and the new borders of Coldfall Wood were set, now encompassing a fraction of their former area. Century-old oaks had been felled, driveways had replaced woodbanks and coppice stools had given way to well-pruned roses. But, at the same time, acorns buried by jays, pockets of wood anemone rhizomes, or bluebell corms may have survived unmolested. Here, outlying refuges of woodland species can still appear in less manicured gardens and large woodland trees cast their shade over adjoining back gardens, allowing lucky local residents to feel more closely attuned to forest dwelling than most Londoners.

51.593578, -0.15747

MUSWELL HILL

The loss of Coldfall Wood's southern half coincided with the development of Muswell Hill, a fine Edwardian suburb affording excellent views over the city. Once a scattered village that grew up around a spring – the 'Mossy Well' – Muswell Hill is perched, like the city's other hilltop settlements, on a gravel cap over the expanse of lower-lying London Clay. It is now a prosperous, if somewhat badly connected quarter, and feels like a place slightly apart. Even the weather can be different up here: biting winter winds cut through more severely than at lower altitudes, rare London snow can last longer, and on hot, humid days, it feels fresher. From its elevated position, some of north London's finest views over the broad Thames Valley, from the City east to Stratford and beyond, open up. The skies expand for miles,

51.589743, -0.1441603

and London can appear like a series of theatrical painted scenes, each describing another level of distance. First, the leafy dip of Crouch End clustered around the modernist, Scandinavian-inspired tower of Hornsey Town Hall culminates in a foliaged edge – the ridge between Highgate Hill and Crouch End Hill. Beyond, the turrets of three competing high-rise neighbourhoods – Stratford, Canary Wharf and the City – define the next level, and in the far distance, the green chalk hills where London finally meets Kent and Surrey complete the vista.

Muswell Hill's streets were laid out to appeal to various shades of Edwardian upward mobility, from the grandeur of Queens and Princes Avenues to the relative modesty of streets such as Halliwick or Ellington Roads. All the houses, whether terraces, semi-detached family homes or large villas have front and rear gardens. Unlike the paved-over yards of car-crazy Barnet, Muswell Hill boasts a verdant and more-or-less continuous forest fringe consisting of mature gardens and, in many places, impressive street trees. Vehicles remain abundant, though, and brash, powerful trophy cars do sometimes screech down the broad avenues unimpeded by speed bumps. But at least here the cars are mostly parked on the street rather than in former front gardens, and so the forest is able to reach pavement edges, creating a shady, walkable feel.

Judging by the number of pedestrians and thriving shops, it's a prosperous environment that encourages community. Largely residential and perennially desirable, Muswell Hill has remained remarkably intact and now represents one of the most impressive and greenest Edwardian suburbs anywhere in London. It was predominantly built in the space of a decade leading up to 1905 by developers who put trees at the heart of their streetscapes. Planted at consistent 25-foot intervals, many of these avenue trees remain, now over a century old. They are London planes, the most frequent choice for the period. Broad, well-proportioned Queens Avenue is typical, retaining many of its original trees that cast welcome shade, moderating temperatures on hot days. However, on the misleadingly named Firs Avenue, less imposing than Queens Avenue, smaller houses sit closer to a much narrower street and the planes have less room. Their crowns have been kept smaller over decades through frequent pollarding, but despite this intensive management regime, girths have predictably and inexorably expanded and in places the navigable pavement area has been reduced so much that buggy-pushing mums can barely pass unhindered. Much the same is happening along Grand Avenue. In places, the local authority – responsible for maintaining the trees – has taken action. Where planes have disappeared, perhaps through death, health and safety concerns or a run-in with a delivery van, they either haven't been replaced or, worse, have been substituted with a different species. Leaving a clearly visible gap at least allows for a young plane to be planted in the future, but in some places – on Birchwood Avenue for instance – wholly inappropriate young rowans or mountain ashes have been put in. Rowans may provide a useful food source for wintering birds, but they're small trees lasting a mere 30 years or so and never attain the grandeur of London planes.

In retrospect, planes may not have been the best choice for these more modest streets. Their Edwardian developers could never have realised how large the trees would grow or how congested with parked cars they would become in the twenty-first century. And the developers were, after all, speculators, their immediate concern was ensuring that the ambience of the new street matched the aspirations of the buyers. Other streets in Muswell Hill have been clear felled of their original closely ordered planes and replaced with a sparse and motley collection of smaller street trees that, on Windermere Road, for instance, includes birches, cherry plums and even a Turkish hazel. By comparison, though, it's Grand Avenue's large trees that make it appear altogether more green and special. Presumably its residents find it an appealing place to live: the characterful plane trees dispense quiet calm while also silently absorbing pollution. In a less car-congested future – perhaps nearer than we might think – pavements could become wider, allowing more space for the large trees that remain and Windermere Road's original plane avenue to be restored.

Just off the main metropolis-bound Muswell Hill Road in and out of the enclave, an entrance to the northern section of the Parkland Walk opens up. Like New York's High Line, the Parkland Walk is a former railway track – parts of which were still in use until 1970 – that has been open to the public since the 1980s. From Muswell Hill to Cranley Gardens, it dives through deep embankments and crosses a former viaduct offering spectacular views over the city. Now a local nature reserve managed by volunteers, it has undergone a remarkable

51.588701, -0.148834

51.5986515, -0.1426529

51.59049, -0.14014

transformation from trim railway land to linear woodland over the last five decades. Despite the large numbers of human hikers, joggers and cyclists, along with all their companion species, most visibly dogs, this new woodland is a haven for a diverse array of plants and animals. Many types of bird can be spotted, including colourful goldcrests and jays, while blackcaps, wrens and song thrushes are less visible but often heard. Twenty-two species of butterfly have been recorded here, including comma, speckled wood and the rarely seen purple hairstreak, which resides high in the canopies of oak trees. The wildlife now present has mostly arrived of its own accord, some of it native, including oak and ash, and some not, such as sycamore and false acacia.

As well as transporting people and goods, railway lines act as wildlife corridors enabling the spread of nature. Take a look at any London railway line bordered by a continuous narrow strip of no man's land and the range of plants may be surprising. These fenced-off, frequently cut-back reserves stretch for many miles, and are vital for connecting natural populations. Butterflies dance through shrubby holm oaks and, on larger edgeland parcels far enough from the tracks to avoid the chainsaws of TfL or Network Rail, trees are allowed to reach their potential. In the nineteenth century, it was the growing Victorian railway networks and their newly disturbed environs that allowed buddleia – that unruly bush with butterfly-attracting purple flower spikes in high summer – to begin its colonisation. It's now one of the first plants to appear in any untended London nook. Other plants and animals have since followed, including muntjac deer, tree of heaven and Japanese knotweed. Vilified by many, Japanese knotweed – once a popular garden plant for herbaceous borders – can march along untended ground, smothering all before it. However, in Japan, where millennia of coexistence with other species has balanced its position in the ecosystem, its roots are a valued source of the dietary supplement resveratrol and in the US, Japanese expatriates seek it out as a food source. Perhaps urban foragers should conduct culinary experiments here, too.

HIGHGATE WOOD TO ARCHWAY

The Parkland Walk emerges at Cranley Gardens, a cherry tree-lined boulevard, quintessentially suburban and infamous as the site of some of serial killer Dennis Nilsen's grisly murders (at number 23D). From here, it's not long before you reach the entrance to Highgate Wood, another ancient woodland remnant, twice the size of Coldfall and much more visited. Like Coldfall, Highgate is a mix of oak and hornbeam with scatterings of other trees – wild service and midland hawthorn, plus more holly and beech. The hornbeams are larger than those at Coldfall, suggesting coppicing has not been carried out for well over a century in much of the wood. The woodland floor is similarly devoid of ground flora and it is possible to feel lost in the denser parts where twisted hornbeams take on a mysterious, otherworldly quality. Skirting through the wood parallel to the busy Muswell Hill Road on the Capital Ring path, it seems astonishing that this tranquil refuge has persisted for so long so close to the city centre.

After an all-too-brief sojourn, the Capital Ring – another circular walk around the city, but much shorter than the London Loop – exits Highgate Wood to cross the road into neighbouring Queen's Wood, also an ancient woodland remnant. Our path, however, misses this gem to emerge near the Woodman pub, which was named in 1828, no doubt after the men who worked the woodlands, and marks the junction with the A1 Archway Road. Just before it, though, a path off Wood Lane runs behind Highgate tube station cutting through a tiny parcel of secondary woodland. Formerly railway land, it has been left to its own devices for at least 50 years, evolving into a dense woodland of vigorous sycamore, ash and ivy that offers a glimpse of what London might look like in the future if nature were given free rein. Here the vegetation is very different from the vision of the past exemplified by ancient Coldfall and Highgate Woods. Those semi-natural woodlands may never have been anything other than that since the last ice age, shaped principally by climate fluctuations and human influence. Certainly those who worked them for millennia would have had different priorities at different times – animal feed, game, construction timber, firewood and charcoal – and these may have impacted on their management, and therefore, their composition. In London it is unlikely that woodland resembling

51.58618, -0.14713

51.5782, -0.14697

41

Highgate or Coldfall could emerge without centuries of human intervention.

At Highgate tube, the Northern Line has disappeared into its tunnel and, unlike at the more northerly stations preceding it, there's no commuter car park. The centre of London is getting closer. Until the early nineteenth century the Great North Road, the principal route from London to Edinburgh, had to struggle through old Highgate Village perched on top of the last ridge of gravel-topped high ground. Some of the finest panoramic views of the green city are to be found here, and it's no surprise that it has been a popular and well-to-do address for centuries. In 1813, the Archway Road was built to slice through this final hurdle and take much of the traffic away from the village. The Archway viaduct was built over the new road to carry the old Hornsey Lane, which remains a narrow road with a faint country feel to it today. This meandering lane marks the last flicker of a quieter, less urban city, but the streetwise urban forest ahead is all the more remarkable.

Below the bridge, Archway Road briefly widens to a dual carriageway, a reminder of a 1970s battle briefly lost, but ultimately won, to abandon a plan to turn the A1 into an expressway. In the 1960s blueprints had been drawn up for a series of four concentric motorway ring roads around London, the innermost known as the Motorway Box. Small parts of it were constructed before a group of activists known as Homes Before Roads successfully reversed the plan, along with the pollution and destruction to swathes of London it would have wrought. Today, such a plan would be unthinkable and no doubt political suicide, but these lower reaches of the Archway Road act as reminders of how development in the city, the environment and urban dwellers' quality of life are intrinsically linked.

HOLLOWAY ROAD TO HIGHBURY FIELDS

Beyond Archway, the busy Holloway Road takes the strain, bearing little resemblance to the bucolic path its name suggests. Found across southern England as well as further afield, ancient 'hollow ways' are deeply cut sunken lanes with earthen banks on either side covered by a canopy of trees to complete a sleepy, tunnel-like effect. Some date back to before Roman times, while others are merely medieval. They may have developed as lanes between property boundary banks, as livestock-droving tracks, or simply as roads worn deep into the land by centuries of weather and traffic. The origins of the Holloway Road, though, are mysterious – one alternative theory has it down as a 'Hallow' way, a pilgrims' path. Undoubtedly, it has been an important route into London for centuries, not least for beasts herded to Smithfield for slaughter and sale. Even a few centuries ago, livestock must have arrived in such numbers and the traffic leaving the city must have been so heavy that any semblance of a rural hollow way would have been unimaginable. Accounts of main roads in the 1700s suggest it would have been a dirty, noisy and smelly thoroughfare whose width would sometimes be immense, depending on how passable the weather allowed it to be.

Just off the main road, though, it was a different story. Before the Victorian residential developments of Holloway, Highbury and Tufnell Park, market gardens and orchards that would have fed the city were common round here and the boundaries determined over centuries or even millennia are now preserved in the Victorian street pattern. Developers laying out the new neighbourhoods found it easy to put roads where the dividing lines between fields once lay, a scheme repeated in nineteenth-century street plans throughout the city. Today, fruit trees remain a frequent component of the urban forest in these parts, although the favoured varieties of apple, pear and cherry are largely ornamental. One street, however, is famed locally for its unusual fruit trees. St John's Villas is lined with sand pears, also known as nashi pears, from Asia and each year they produce large russet, apple-like fruit loved by the culinarily adventurous and loathed by less sure-footed residents. In recent years, Islington council has kept the trees on a short pruning leash, ensuring fruit is never abundant, and is on hand each autumn to pluck the meagre crop before it descends to coat pavements with pear smoothie or dent shining Audis.

At the southern end of the Holloway Road lies Highbury Corner. Built in the 1960s after the site was flattened by a V1 rocket in June 1944, the redevelopment included an arboretum containing an intriguing array of now mature trees. According to one former Islington tree officer, it was planted as an experiment to determine the resilience of new species to city life, and perhaps also partly as a memorial to the

51.565219, -0.130331

51.545839, -0.102684

26 people who lost their lives in the wartime rocket attack. Among the international collection of trees found here are a southern beech from Chile, several maples and a striking array of conifers from around the world. Road layout changes mean the former roundabout is accessible through its connection to Upper Street by a pedestrian isthmus incorporating new trees.

A stone's throw from the arboretum is the largest park in Islington, London's most densely populated borough. At just 11.5 hectares, Highbury Fields may be small by London standards, but is, nevertheless, packed with interest. Laid out in 1886, it contains 200 plane trees which, at more than 130 years old, are in their prime. But this is no monoculture. The planes are surprisingly different – the legacy of Victorian park developers who, it is thought, sourced the 200 trees from several suppliers, who each provided different cultivars of the same species. Some have knobbly trunks, others are smoother; some have very indented leaves while others are much less so. The varietals' original names are now forgotten – perhaps their propagators never thought to give them any – but researchers are beginning to categorise them and have identified 'Westminster' and 'Hackney' forms here. Other distinctive plane trees can be found elsewhere in London and just up the Holloway Road, St Mary Magdalene Garden is another refuge for old planes. Here the 'Pyramidalis' cultivar is frequent and the garden is home to one of the largest examples in London. Despite its lofty name, though, it's a relatively short and spreading type.

51.548229, -0.108467

UPPER STREET TO AMWELL STREET

Turning down Upper Street, towards Islington Green, a range of roadside trees shades the pavement. Opposite the Town Hall stands a fine row of large North American honey locusts, a species that has been in and out of fashion over the last few decades – a fate that tends to befall street trees. The Upper Street row appears to represent an early wave of honey locust planting, perhaps when few cultivars of this naturally thorny tree were available. Most of the common cultivars are thornless, but these ones are armed with great clusters of frightening spikes, some of which are branched for maximum impact. Like the nashi pears in Holloway, the Upper Street thorns are regularly removed.

At Angel, two noteworthy trees are close by. One, a black poplar, hangs over Pentonville Road from the corner of Joseph Grimaldi Park, a former churchyard. The park is named after a famous Regency comic actor and clown associated with nearby Sadler's Wells, whose 1837 grave can be found here. The native black poplar, a distinct subspecies, is noteworthy as one of the rarest British trees – only around 7,000 exist. It's difficult to say how it arrived in the park. The species is normally associated with floodplains and river banks, so it was most likely planted back in the churchyard days. It has been much pollarded, making it difficult to age, but the bark is cracked and irregular, suggesting a long stint next to the busy road. This is the species that gave the East End neighbourhood of Poplar its name – a reminder that the Thames was once un-embanked and lined with huge black poplars. This vision is still intact at Barnes where a handful of mature trees can be seen by the river. Native black poplars should not be confused with the similar and more common poplars found throughout London. Our native tree – a problematic term meaning its pollen has been recorded in deposits from just after the last ice age when Britain still had a land connection to the continent – is less regularly shaped than the much more frequently planted species.

The other roadside tree to admire nearby is known as the Amwell Fig. It is a huge three-trunked specimen wider than it is tall and propped up behind a fence outside the Clerkenwell Parochial School on Amwell Street, which lies between Pentonville Road and Rosebery Avenue. This is one of the 61 Great Trees of London, a list of historic trees drawn up by the charity Trees for Cities. It is thought the fig dates to the building of the school in 1828 and may have been planted to help illustrate Biblical stories for the pupils – perhaps apple trees were once present in this Garden of Eden, too. Fig trees are found in unexpected places throughout London, and while often associated with church buildings, they can also be found on railway embankments and other edgelands. While the fruits rarely ripen in the capital, enough imported figs are consumed – and discarded – here that the trees can easily seed themselves. This opportunistic habit illustrates a frequent method for plant dispersal – hitching a ride with passing animals, in this case, us humans. Apples and other fruits are thought to have arrived in Europe from central Asia through a similar process of witting, or unwitting, human-aided distribution.

SMITHFIELD TO THE BARBICAN

Turning into elegant Rosebery Avenue from Amwell Street can be
a relief in summer, its high canopy of plane trees acting to shade
passers-by. This is an eminently walkable thoroughfare. At its eastern
end, St John's Street heads south towards the City, where the most
southerly section of the Great North Road ends at Smithfield. Crossing
the treeless confines of Smithfield Market can be a daunting prospect
with huge refrigerated lorries – replacing the livestock herds of previous
centuries – from Scotland, Ireland, France and further afield delivering
carcasses to the only central London market still functioning as it
was intended. It's surely only a matter of time before developers and,
perhaps, increasing vegetarianism force the meat market to relocate.
Such a scenario would open a rare opportunity to introduce greenery
to Smithfield, perhaps for the first time in its existence. An ancient
model for how the urban forest might one day extend to this clearing
exists nearby in the shape of The Charterhouse, a rambling complex
of buildings including almshouses, a chapel and medical school all
surrounded by gardens, lawns and many large trees. Much of the
complex is private, but a magnificent arboreal spectacle can be seen
each summer in early July from Clerkenwell Road when, from behind a
high ivy-clad brick wall, the sparkling canopy of a large golden rain tree
is visible – take a bus along the street for a top-deck view. Also known
as pride of India (a misleading name as the tree originates from east
Asia), the species provides interest all year round. Throughout winter
prominent brown seed pods persist and in spring coral pink leaves
appear. Then in high summer, when few other trees are blooming,
the flowers arrive: masses of tiny bright yellow petals that give a head-
turning stardust effect – the golden rain.

     Our trail concludes in the Barbican, the high-spec, high-
modernist concrete super estate incorporating cultural institutions such
as the Barbican Art Gallery and Concert Hall, and the Guildhall School
of Music and Drama. The Barbican represents the optimistic, visionary
architecture of the 1960s and '70s, elevating visitors and residents intel-
lectually and physically above the capital's bustle and dirt. A masterful
concept of how to live in a city – even the flats were finished with
bespoke kitchens and bathrooms – the Barbican's brutal aesthetics rely

on straight lines and unadorned concrete, but nature is at the heart
of its design. Cars and traffic noise are left behind at ground level,
and their absence means the pace on the vast concrete savannah-like
podium is slowed to human speed. At its centre, the estate is built
around a rectangular lake and a mini forest glade. Gilbert House,
a residential block on concrete columns, floats high above the lake,
like something out of a science-fiction utopia. But this modernist
vision most definitely speaks of humankind's domination over nature –
everything is ordered and compartmentalised and nature always plays
second fiddle to architecture. It is barely conceivable that anything like
the Barbican could be built now, not least because its development
was predicated on wartime destruction. It should be thought of as an
expression of mid-twentieth-century idealism and an evolutionary step
in how we might consider living together with nature.

51.519157, -0.093143

Entering the Barbican complex from its tube station, most
people pass by oblivious to a somewhat lumpen tree stump lurking in
the shadows. This is Mendelssohn's Tree – the remains of a tree that
fell in Burnham Beeches in Buckinghamshire, an amazing tract of
ancient forest largely comprised of very old pollarded beeches. It was in
this forest, and in particular, under this tree, that the German composer
of the 'Scottish Symphony', Felix Mendelssohn, conceived several of
his most famous orchestral works while on his frequent visits to Britain.
Burnham Beeches is owned by the City of London Corporation, a
significant landowner of woodlands and open spaces around the capital,
and when the 500-year-old tree eventually fell in 1990, a section of it
was, somewhat inexplicably, preserved and transported to the Barbican.

51.520356, -0.096917

▲

ERITH
TO
CANARY
WHARF

▼

ERITH TO BELVEDERE VILLAGE

The estuarine settlement of Erith lies just upstream from where the
River Darent joins the Thames and Kent borders London. Until 1965,
Erith was part of Kent, but local government reorganisation moved
it into the London borough of Bexley and turned it into a remote city
suburb. The capital's skyscrapers are out of sight here and instead an
industrial vista of modern factories, warehouses, electricity pylons and
wind turbines opens up. Not far downriver, the suspended span of the
Dartford Crossing and the soaring concrete chimney of Littlebrook
Power Station are the tallest structures around. On the opposite bank,
a prominent ridge swarming with gulls dominates. This is the Rainham
landfill site. Covering 177 hectares, it takes in 1.5 million tonnes of
London's waste every year and has been operating for a century and a
half. Over that time, what was once low-lying salt marsh has now built
up into an artificial hill, rather like a Middle Eastern tell, only here the
process has taken a mere 150 years rather than millennia. When future
geologists investigate this human-made mound the strata it contains
will reveal rich deposits of processed materials from across the globe.
How it will be interpreted is anybody's guess. At some point the site
will finally be capped and closed to new deposits and, like other
former landfill sites, will presumably become an open space. After
all, who would want to live or work on a potentially toxic hill? But
over time, nature will surely recolonise and riverside woodland
may once again take hold.

Just downstream from Erith, past the yacht club, a <u>riverside
path</u> skirts through the otherwise flat salt-marsh landscape. Here,
at low tide, beyond the rushes and stunted hawthorns, the Thames
foreshore reveals something astonishing: the stumps of a Neolithic
wood that have been preserved in the mud and salt water for the last
5,000 years. So far, 18 types of tree and shrub have been identified here
and archaeologists speculate that alder was the most common tree in
the last area of woodland to occupy the spot. But at some point prior to
that, perhaps when water levels were lower, it was yew that dominated,
and findings from other sites suggest yew was abundant all along the
river as far upstream as Blackwall. This ancient riverside forest must
have been quite a sight: deep, dark and decidedly unwelcoming to
river-borne visitors or would-be colonisers. Now, yew is rarely, if ever,
associated with riverbanks, and almost never a dominant woodland
tree. Kingley Vale in Sussex is a very rare yew wood: impenetrable and,
it seems, unassailable – how could another species get a foothold in
its evergreen gloom? It's possible yew woods were once much more
common than they are now. The trees are poisonous to livestock so they
may have been systematically removed by Neolithic people in favour
of types more prized for animal forage, such as oak or beech.

Not far from Erith's waterfront lies <u>St John the Baptist</u>, the
town's thirteenth-century parish church. Its sprawling grounds are
home to a yew tree but, while elderly, it certainly isn't Neolithic, nor
anywhere near as old as the church. Like many London churchyards,
it shows signs of having been neglected in its past. Large sycamores
– pioneers of untended ground in London – abound and another
twin-trunked yew casually sprouts from a nineteenth-century grave.

Leaving the church and up overgrown steps to a <u>pedestrian
bridge</u>, the path crosses a dual carriageway – the Bronze Age Way –
and beyond the ground starts to rise. This is the eastern end of the great
wooded ridge that stretches west across south-east London to Shooters
Hill. Dominating this corner of the capital, the tree-cloaked gravel
upland can be seen from many vantage points around the city, even
from the far northern heights of High Barnet (p31). The woods are little
known, but they're a significant feature, serving to separate the grittier,
riverside settlements from more genteel suburbs such as Bexleyheath,
Chislehurst and Bromley on the landward side. Looking like a fat green

finger poking almost to Greenwich, they have defied developers
for centuries and are worthy of greater protection and celebration.

At the end of Valley Road, the Green Chain Walk – part of
a network of paths running through the boroughs of Bexley,
Greenwich and Bromley – enters Frank's Park. Named after
industrialist-turned-philanthropist Frank Beadle, who stumped up the
cash for the local authority to buy the grounds of Belvedere House
in 1920, the park is little known outside its immediate vicinity. It's
an impressive example of secondary woodland – one that naturally
generates from sites that haven't always been home to trees. Formerly
the grounds of a big house, it must have been laid out as aristocratic
gardens in its heyday, featuring patches of woodland and isolated trees,
while commanding fine views over the Thames and beyond. Now,
though, the woodland has increased and matured to cover much of the
park and is home to some remarkable, elderly individual trees. Near the
Valley Road entrance a huge field maple holds its own among mature
oaks and towering sweet chestnuts. Field maple is not usually thought
of as a woodland tree – its alternative name of hedge maple reflects its
more common habitat. Elsewhere, one or two big old horse chestnuts
are also to be found, as well as beech – one elephantine tree on the
park's north-western edge could be 200 years old.

Surprisingly, beech is not common in London. Although one of
the most beautiful big trees, nervous urban foresters have long worried
about its shallow roots and mountains of beech nuts and, as a result, it
has rarely been planted here. Beech leaves are some of the last to appear
in spring, but when they do, they're a dazzling fresh green. In a mast year
– when trees produce seeds in unusual abundance – beech nuts will start
raining down through the canopy from late summer. It can be a dramatic
phenomenon, with woody nuts tumbling gently from high branches for
weeks, creating a noisy cascade as leaves break their fall. But beech trees
are under threat. London's growing population of grey squirrels strip
their bark, causing younger trees to ail and in some cases die, effectively
halting their regeneration. Since their introduction from North America
in the early twentieth century, grey squirrels have completely
outcompeted the resident red squirrels, pushing them out of the city.

Leaving Frank's Park, Halt Robin Road marks the northern edge
of Belvedere village. Here the street pattern appears to follow former

51.487377, 0.165988

51.487593, 0.164715

51.488739, 0.157773

51.488888, 0.153759

paths and defines the boundaries of what may once have been woods or heathland between the park and Lesnes Abbey Woods. The journey along the ridge provides views over the plain below to the river and Dagenham beyond. Pressure on land feels less intense in this part of town despite, or perhaps because of, the industry strung out for miles along both banks of the Thames. There is more breathing space than in London's more densely populated neighbourhoods where land values ensure every inch is accounted for and, though this high ground is relatively affluent, it is not yet a millionaires' enclave. That said, its attractive leafiness means it could just be a matter of time.

LESNES ABBEY WOODS

The Green Chain Walk enters Lesnes Abbey Woods via a narrow corridor of trees bounded by houses to the north and allotments to the south. These much-prized parcels of land appear to have been carved out of the woodland many decades ago and, like allotments elsewhere in the city, are well-tended. Increasingly sought after by green-fingered Londoners, these oases of small-scale metropolitan agriculture have grown fewer and fewer in number and new ones are virtually non-existent. Allotment gardening has become a leisure activity enjoyed by a minority, but as London's population grows, and ever more high-rise apartment blocks are built, urban gardening may become an ever-more important way to foster communities and connect people with the food they eat. New developments with attached allotments or forest gardens could one day prove to be highly sought after, just as houses on tree-lined avenues appear to be more desirable – and valuable – than those on treeless roads.

Lesnes Abbey Woods have a unique character. Different from the dark ancient woods of north London, their plural name provides a clue to their patchwork nature. Covering a relatively large area – 88 hectares – and mixing ancient woodland, heathland and secondary woodland, their structure is significantly influenced by the underlying geology, stretching across a multitude of marked dips and troughs over the high ground. Much of the surface geology is sandy with pebbles – the Blackheath Beds – although there are also areas of more neutral clay and alkaline chalk. The woods contain important fossil

51.489086, 0.142941

beds, too: Eocene epoch deposits from around 54 million years
ago frequently give up fossilised shark teeth. Animals, including
humans, have dug, or rather, scratched at the surface of these ancient
woods for millennia – for shelter, food and mineral resources – but
have not drastically altered the subtle relief of undulating ground.
There is little legacy of human-made structures, agriculture or
horticulture; dips and mounds have not been levelled, and soils
have been left to gradually accumulate undisturbed. These ancient
woodlands represent a direct living connection to times past, with a
prehistoric lineage going back to the wildwood tamed by bronze-age
Londoners who perhaps knew the Erith riverside forest. For us today,
they are at once complex living systems, museums and laboratories,
as well as places of calm, beauty and joy.

    The highest ground at Lesnes Abbey Woods is <u>acid heathland</u>,
a type of habitat that, counterintuitively, is also known as lowland heath
to differentiate it from the moorlands of northern and western Britain.
It feels old and little visited – in general, these woods seems bigger,
rougher and wilder than the more manicured spaces further north.
The plateau comprises open woodland with oaks and shrubby rowans
interspersed with heather, gorse, bracken and grasses. The sparse oaks
are stunted and twisted – suggesting slow and difficult growth – and
there are signs that they have been coppiced in the past with multiple
trunks branching near to the ground. Surveying this landscape from the
hump of what is signposted as a tumulus – a bronze-age burial mound –
you feel a long way from London. The woods are dense enough to block
out views, no roads impinge and only the noise of the City Airport-bound
planes following the Thames are there to remind you that this is the
twenty-first century.

    It's during springtime, before the trees come into leaf, that
Lesnes Abbey Woods are at their most glorious. This is when the wild
daffodils bloom. The woods are London's best and perhaps only spot to
see these flowers in a natural setting. Wild daffodils are a smaller, more
delicate version of the familiar yellow garden varieties and when you
see these elegant originals you might wonder why horticulturalists have
bothered trying to 'improve' on them. The daffodils are followed by
bluebells and throughout early spring the white stars of wood anemone
also cover swathes of the woodland floor.

51.486722, 0.136663

All along the ridge from Frank's Park, particularly at this eastern end, you find sweet chestnut, a species almost absent from the north London urban forest. With its large, glossy leaves, it can look quite exotic in an English wood, but is common across much of Kent, Sussex and Essex and has been harvested as coppice for centuries – at one time, the poles used in Kentish hop gardens were exclusively chestnut. However, it is absent from prehistoric pollen records so, technically, is not native. That said, unlike the grey squirrel or vilified Japanese knotweed, sweet chestnut has not caused problems for the other species with which it now cohabits. It's not known exactly when it arrived, but it's thought the Romans may have imported it, or at least its seeds, to supplement legionnaires' diets. Like figs and apples, chestnuts hitched a ride with travelling humans and have now been happily settled here for thousands of years. The species is thought to be native to the Balkans, but is found much further afield today. Sweet chestnut forests are frequent in France and Spain where their wood and nuts are prized, and while British trees do produce edible nuts, most roasted chestnut vendors on Oxford Street peddle larger continental morsels.

The large coppice stools in Lesnes Abbey attest to the fact that wood was once harvested here but, as in north London, no coppicing has been carried out for decades, save for a few pockets of small-scale conservation cutting. Maybe it's time to think again about coppicing woodland on our doorstep. Efforts to curb plastic use and higher shipping costs might soon make the economics of locally produced, sustainable woodland products – from packaging to garden furniture – more attractive to Londoners.

Unobtrusive signposts and interpretation boards help guide visitors around the area, which also include the ruins of <u>Lesnes Abbey</u>, after which the woods and the nearby settlement of Abbey Wood are named. Located on the woods' northern fringe where the land starts descending to meet the Thames floodplain, the ruined twelfth-century abbey offers fine views upriver to Canary Wharf and the City. On the lawn in front of what remains of the northern wall, grows a gnarled and recumbent <u>black mulberry</u>, a tree we perhaps tend to venerate more than others. Another species that followed human settlements, it's thought to originate from what is now Iran, its precise native distribution now lost in the mists of time. Resembling blackberries,

51.488706, 0.128756

51.489310, 0.128773

ripe mulberries are sweetly delicious and need to be eaten straight off the tree. They're so delicate that you'll never see them on supermarket shelves, making them a rare and seasonal treat – August and September – but one that's free for those in the know. A word of warning: very ripe mulberries ooze staining red juice, so to avoid being literally 'caught red-handed', would-be scrumpers should seek the tree owner's permission before helping themselves.

Something of a royal mistake, mulberries have been frequent in London since the early seventeenth century when they were planted at the behest of James I, who planned to energise the economy by starting an English silk industry. Silkworms – moth caterpillars whose larval stage cocoon is the source of silk thread – feed exclusively on mulberry leaves, but for reasons that are still a matter of speculation, James introduced black mulberries, a tree not much favoured by the picky caterpillars, who turn their noses up at anything other than white mulberry leaves. Consequently, London's homegrown Jacobean silk industry never took off. White mulberry trees are found in London, though. They are much rarer than their black cousins, but can be seen in parks or as occasional street trees. Their fruits look similar to black mulberries but, as their name implies, are usually lighter in colour. They are also less juicy and – in London at least – have an inferior taste.

The Lesnes Abbey mulberry looks ancient, and that's their trick: they can appear old, but they're often younger than they seem – this one might only be 200 years or so. As mulberries age, their branches gradually succumb to gravity and, as is the case here, the trees become considerably broader than they are tall. Here, near-horizontal limbs, protected behind a fence, are propped up in a vain attempt to slow their inevitable decline.

Re-entering the woods, the path climbs up the ridge once more, passing one of several carved tree trunks. All too frequent in semi-natural areas, ill-advised wooden sculptures or crude woodland furniture carved from felled or dead timber seem inappropriate in such wild surroundings. Well-meaning proxies for forgotten woodland crafts, they just cannot compete with the abject beauty of a blasted oak, the curiousness of a naturally misshapen chestnut bole, or the sublime refraction of sunlight through leaves and branches. They might be considered an expression of man's dominion over the forest,

51.487388, 0.127873

a kind of sanctioned but futile vandalism to remind the ecosystem who's in charge.

Moving on, the path starts to level as it crosses <u>New Road</u>, a lane through the woods, and crosses the boundary between the boroughs of Bexley and Greenwich where the woodland continues under a new name: Bostall Heath.

BOSTALL HEATH TO SHOULDER OF MUTTON GREEN

The mosaic of wood, parks and heaths crosses many borders as it pushes its way into the city. As Lesnes Abbey Woods become Bostall Heath, new and ominous signs announce the change of jurisdiction. Gone is the informative low-key signage of Bexley; here in Greenwich boards show diagrammatic maps of three distinct areas, each colour coded and split into smaller, numbered squares – Green 19 or Gold 6, for instance. They're to help us locate ourselves should we need to call the emergency services, it's explained. We must be entering truly wild London now.

The heathland here has reverted to woodland. Without grazing livestock or active intervention to keep the vegetation at bay, the same would happen to heaths and moors across the country. These types of habitat are human made, but are not intensively managed or disturbed and are part of an ancient tapestry of land use. Like chalk downland, heaths are important for a range of specialist plants and animals. The rare, but possibly overlooked Dartford warbler, a small greyish-brown bird with red rings around its eyes, takes its name from some specimens that were shot between Dartford and Bexleyheath in 1773. It is now long gone from these parts, but Bostall Heath may once have played host to these drably iconic little birds.

Crossing from Bostall Heath to <u>Bostall Wood</u>, more signs urge vigilance – this time because of two newly arrived woodland menaces: the oak processionary moth and sweet chestnut blight, both of which have been sighted locally. The oak processionary moth made it to west London in 2006, having migrated with a warming climate from southern Europe, and has established itself far beyond since. Harmless to trees, the moth's marching caterpillars are the problem, parading en masse around oak trunks and branches. Their minute toxic hairs are highly irritating to other animals, including humans, and can cause an allergic reaction if touched or inhaled. Sweet chestnut blight, on the other hand, is a tree killer, first recognised not far from London in 2011. It's a fungus that causes chestnut trees to wilt, lose branches and, ultimately, die.

How do we make sense of these and other scourges lining up to harm our trees or make life miserable for those of us who enjoy the forest? It sometimes seems there's little we can do, but understanding the problems, and thinking about how we're all entangled in the ecosystem could lead to positive changes. Nature is a system of which we're all a part. We may not be in charge of it, but we certainly can and do influence it and, as our population expands, our impact increases. The case of sweet chestnut blight may be instructive. It's a disease caused by a fungus attacking the bark and effectively strangling the tree. It evolved in east Asia along with a species of sweet chestnut closely related to the European species, but because host and pathogen evolved together, the Asian trees do not suffer the same extreme symptoms as those here. As global trade has steadily increased over the last few hundred years, the exchange of organic material – and its hangers-on – has also risen. Species that evolved in an ecosystem in one part of the world can easily find themselves in new ecosystems on a completely different continent. Most of the time, these new arrivals fail to flourish, but every now and again, a certain environment offers unmissable opportunities for one to thrive and multiply. Sweet chestnut blight got to North America in the early twentieth century through infected timber imported from China and it wrought havoc. The local American chestnut was highly susceptible – more so than our own – and within a few decades an estimated 3.5 billion trees had been destroyed. American chestnuts were the most frequent tree in the eastern US, but today little sign of this once-dominant species remains. The story has been repeated many times (think Dutch elm disease) and will go on repeating as pests and diseases affecting other, often localised, species follow our globalised trade routes.

But we can learn from past mistakes and change our behaviour. If we are to import exotic plant species, we must assume responsibility and, as with animals, observe quarantine controls before letting them out into the broader environment. But perhaps the most obvious actions we can take is that we ensure wherever possible we use locally sourced materials, plants and seeds whose provenance we can be sure of. We may be the species that hunted the last mammoths and cut down wildwoods, but we are also the one that has opposed destructive road building and established the green belt. Maybe the tide is slowly beginning to turn and, by taking small actions as individuals, we can make a difference.

Back in the eighteenth century, Bostall Woods, like much of the neighbouring woodland, were still remote, large and dense enough to be the hideout of highwaymen who preyed on traffic travelling along the nearby Dover Road. According to popular eighteenth- and nineteenth-century accounts, a feature known as Turpin's Cave on the edge of the wood was the refuge of that most famous of highwaymen, Dick Turpin. This romanticised tale is probably wishful thinking – Turpin is more accurately associated with Epping Forest where there's another Turpin's Cave – but that doesn't diminish the feelings of eeriness and danger the forest can evoke. As the signs suggest, Bostall Woods can feel remote even today. Here, a few miles from the centre of London, you can enter the woods, leave the city behind and feel quite alone. You'll find no CCTV and no phone signal in the depths; you also rarely encounter other people – and those you do meet may not all be dog walkers or wild food foragers. With its winding, criss-crossing paths and lack of signposts stoking confusion, it's not unimaginable to think there might still be fugitives lurking in here.

Leaving Bostall Woods, the sense of unease is heightened by the sight of Plumstead Cemetery, complete with its gothic entrance and funereal conifers. The Foresters Arms across the road offers some relief before the Green Chain Walk continues through East Wickham Open Space and eventually emerges in suburban Welling. The streets here follow a pattern of former land boundaries familiar elsewhere in London, but these are mid-twentieth-century developments, suggesting the woods, heaths and fields may have persisted longer in these parts. Perhaps the exodus of the Dartford warbler was a relatively recent event. Another pub, the appropriately named Green Man, looks to be of a similar age to the houses, but sadly lacks a painted sign showing a wood sprite spewing hawthorn sprigs. Depictions of Green Men – typically male heads half-hidden by foliage – are frequently encountered as carvings or, less commonly, on stained-glass windows in medieval churches. Secular in their conception, they appear to represent the ancient idea of the synthesis of man and forest, perhaps alluding to the rebirth of spring and the fecundity of nature. But there is also another, more painful interpretation: they commemorate the aftermath of the fourteenth-century Black Death, which saw as much as half of the population wiped out. Following the epidemic, labour was scarce and large areas of land, no longer needed for agriculture, was left unworked, giving nature the chance to return and gradually take over newly abandoned farms, fields and villages. The faces of Green Men are mournful and sometimes sinister – they're frequently frowning or in a state of inebriation.

Passing Shoulder of Mutton Green on Wickham Street, a small triangle of grass with a few trees, Bellegrove Road forms a T-junction stretching dead straight to the left and right. This is the old Dover Road – Watling Street – the Roman route linking the channel ports with Londinium (London), Verulamium (St Albans) and beyond. The Romans built their road on a trackway used by the Britons who preceded them. Beyond the mid-century suburbia, tarmac and road markings, the ancient contours and boundaries in this landscape are still evident. This same route has carried Roman armies, Chaucerian pilgrims and Huguenot asylum seekers, as well as commuters and locals, on countless journeys through the forest.

OXLEAS WOODS TO SEVERNDROOG CASTLE

Heading north-west on Bellegrove Road, the houses of Welling soon peter out as Oxleas Woodlands take over on the left. The pavement ends abruptly in line with the last semi, and the entrance to the woods opens up. Just inside, by the side of the leaf litter-covered path, two old iron milestones serve as reminders of London's shifting boundaries, one announcing the 'London County Council Boundary'; the other stating 'Borough of Woolwich 1903'. On the roadside, another sign shows the road has now become Shooters Hill. This is another complex of ancient woodland comprising Oxleas Wood itself, Jack Wood, Oxleas Meadows, Shepherdleas Wood, Falconwood Field, Eltham Park and Eltham Common. Together they mark the end of the great wooded ridge

51.466348, 0.092408
51.465022, 0.092019
51.466560, 0.082297

running from the very edge of London to fare zone 3 and are almost within spitting distance of Blackheath, Greenwich and Lewisham.

Oxleas Wood was the site of one of the last great battles to preserve London's green spaces. In 1993, the government dropped plans to build a motorway through the eastern side of the woods after local residents and environmental campaigners from across the city united against the proposed East London River Crossing. After years of campaigning, organising and objecting to proposals, the anti-road lobbyists won the day and won the argument. A Tory government with a slim majority faced with thousands of protesters in marginal seats preparing to put themselves between the trees and bulldozers finally saw sense. Whether governments have really understood how much people value the environment is difficult to say – nothing as destructive has been mooted since – but what's certain is that the next battle between development and environmental protection will be over something else, perhaps the expansion of Heathrow or the loosening of green belt planning controls.

It's no surprise campaigners battled so passionately to save Oxleas Wood – it's a real gem. Having such a large, magnificent piece of woodland nearby must bring local residents an enormous sense of comfort and wellbeing. A big green block of quietude, come nightfall it also becomes a beacon of darkness in the light-polluted city. But these untold and uncosted benefits may be its Achilles' heel. Unless policy-makers can understand the advantages that woodlands provide to the city and its inhabitants in quantifiable terms, they are always likely to be at risk.

A piece of the countryside in the city, Oxleas provides a home and foothold from which woodland species could potentially multiply. The wood is different from those further east: there is less chestnut here and instead the old oaks rub shoulders with birch, holly, hazel and hornbeam coppice. The enigmatic wild service tree is frequent, too. A rare native of ancient woodlands, wild service is a flowering tree with distinctive leaves and brown berries that become edible after bletting – a softening process beyond ripening that's often kicked off through freezing and unfreezing. Legend has it that the fruits of the wild service were used by the Romans to flavour beer, and its puzzling name evolved from a corruption of the Latin word for beer, 'cerevisia'. It is also known as the chequer, or checker, tree because of the checkerboard appearance of the bark on mature examples – in southern England, pubs called 'Chequers' are likely to be named after it. The easiest way to recognise wild service, though, is by the leaves. Spiky and palmate (hand-like), somewhere between a hawthorn and a maple, they turn golden orange through to scarlet in the autumn. In May, the creamy blossom opens in clusters, similar to that of the related whitebeam and rowan.

Still following the Green Chain Walk, the woods open up on to Oxleas Meadow, a sloping expanse of grass covering an underground reservoir. There's a café here with magnificent views of unbroken countryside framed by trees to the south – a remarkable vista. On the horizon sits the largely wooded rim of the North Downs dotted with open fields, while a gentle wooded slope eases in from the west with houses nestling among the trees. Only a slab block in the middle distance to the south-east – remote Bexley or Bromley – is a reminder of how far into the city these bucolic woods reach.

The highest point of the ridge is the summit of Shooters Hill, the arduous slope out of town from Blackheath that apparently takes its name from the felons who in centuries past regularly unburdened travellers of their valuables, often at gunpoint. As late as the 1700s, condemned criminals were executed here and their corpses were hung from gibbets to act as grisly deterrents to would-be bandits.

Sheltering in woods nearby is the triangular Severndroog Castle, an eighteenth-century belvedere. Lady James of Eltham had the tower built in 1784 to commemorate her husband, Commodore Sir William James. The structure is also a monument to colonialism and a marker in the globalisation timeline: Severndroog is an anglicisation of Suvarnadurg, the Indian fortress where Commodore James made his name and, ultimately, his fortune. In 1755 the forces of the East India Company he was commanding attacked and destroyed Suvarnadurg, paving the way for the consolidation of British power in India and the subsequent flow of goods from the subcontinent. Returning to London, James became a director of the East India Company and an MP. He built an estate, Park Farm Place, in nearby Eltham where he was buried in 1783. Following Lady James's death, Severndroog Castle went through a series of owners and uses until it was eventually restored and opened to the public in 2014.

51.466582, 0.070447

51.469235, 0.066492

51.466674, 0.060053

The castle stands just high enough to overlook the trees, which slope off in all directions. Unobscured for 360 degrees, the view from the top is surely one of the finest in London, particularly on a crisp, clear winter's day. From here, the geography of the capital is laid out before you, with virtually every landmark visible. But what's most striking are the trees. London really is a forest. A seamless leafy canopy covers the city, creating an arboreal inland sea surrounded by low hills, and containing a patchwork of islands – some are glass and concrete pinnacles where buildings break through; others are smaller open spaces, such as nearby Blackheath. Up here, the whole city is comprehensible, right to where it ends and the countryside spreads out beyond. On a clear day, the sharp-eyed can make out Windsor Castle to the far west and the towers of Croydon to the south-west, while to the north there's Alexandra Palace and, in the north-west, Harrow on the Hill and the arch of Wembley Stadium. To the east and south, the chalk hills of Kent and Surrey rise to a definite horizon.

Looking down into the canopy from up here provides an opportunity to see large trees at close range and from an unusual angle. Each one is defined, and yet gaps in the canopy are barely perceptible. Colours change subtly while the character of the foliage morphs, with oaks rubbing up against chestnuts. Rising through the undulations, one particular tree points more defiantly skyward – a <u>giant redwood</u> – situated in the adjacent former grounds of a now-demolished Victorian villa, Castle Wood House, that have now merged with the woods. Giant Redwoods arrived in England from California in the 1850s and immediately became the must-have tree for anyone with the space to accommodate one; for the seriously wealthy, nothing less than an avenue full would suffice. In their restricted native range in the foothills of the Sierra Nevada mountains, giant redwoods live for thousands of years and reach heights of 85 metres or more. This one is at most 160 years old and is already taller than the surrounding trees – it might be just a few years before Severndroog's uninterrupted view is obscured.

ELTHAM COMMON TO CHARLTON HOUSE

From Severndroog Castle, the path leads through the woodland of Eltham Common to the crossroads of Shooters Hill Road and the South Circular where the Green Chain Walk continues into the north-western corner of Woolwich Common. This is an expanse of grassland left to its own devices. Trees have started to close in, but it's mostly scrub with prickly clumps of bramble, hawthorn and black-thorn. Among the spinneys along its edges, a good deal of vigorous, large-leaved thorn is present. Differing from the familiar hawthorn, this is a related North American species, scarlet thorn perhaps. There are countless northern hemisphere hawthorn species and they can be difficult to tell apart. Another American species, the common hawthorn lookalike Washington thorn, is reputed to have naturalised in some parts of London, causing much confusion for botanists. These Woolwich thorns, however, are very different from related native trees and are well established here, not far from the former docks and shipyards of Woolwich, Greenwich and Silvertown.

The path continues through the backstreets of Charlton, eventually arriving at Charlton Park, a prairie-like grassland enclosed within a perimeter of mature lime trees. A ha-ha separates it from the lawns of Charlton House at its western end. Charlton House is an exceptional example of a Jacobean stately home built between 1607 and 1612 for James I's eldest son Henry and his tutor, though the former promptly died just as the house was completed, placing his younger brother Charles – later Charles I – first in line to the throne. It is now owned by Greenwich council and has a very civic feel about it: municipal palm trees spring from begonia beds either side of the front entrance. But hidden in the car park off to the side lies an ancient treasure – another very old mulberry, and this one is even more special than the Lesnes Abbey tree. It could well be the same age as the house, planted during James's ill-fated mulberry boom 400 years ago. Unlike the one in Lesnes Abbey, which although reclining is in rude health, this has all the signs of being very aged – some branches are rotten and limbs appear to have been removed over the years. The overall sense is of a much-diminished specimen, but one that's all the more awe-inspiring in its wizened state. This truly is an

51.472686, 0.055178

51.479291, 0.041182

51.481100, 0.036358

old tree, which has witnessed so much and has a direct connection to London's history and heritage.

Like the Lesnes Abbey tree, it is fenced off and propped up. It's also well decorated with signs. One warns not to climb the branches, but there's seemingly no ban on picking the fruit – though any mulberry fanciers would need to beat the chef at the on-site Charlton Tea Rooms, who serves up mulberry desserts when they're in season. Half-hidden in the undergrowth around the tree's base, other placards provide snippets of information – including the fact that this is one of the Great Trees of London. The oldest sign is shrouded in undergrowth, its paint worn off and a marked fracture almost splitting it in two. It proclaims 'The First Mulberry Tree Planted in England', a fact corroborated by another placard that reads: 'Said to be the first of its species planted in England in 1608'. However, a newer sign outside the fenced-off area puts a question mark over this claim, mentioning recent archaeological finds of Roman-era mulberry seeds. Given that the fruits don't travel, this suggests mulberry trees may well have been present in London over a thousand years before James's seventeenth-century mulberry craze.

CHARLTON TO GREENWICH PARK

Frequent stops to admire mature limes and planes slow progress through the tree-lined suburban avenues of Charlton and Westcombe Park. Then, as you approach the north-east corner of Greenwich Park, the arresting silhouette of a mature cedar of Lebanon in a <u>Vanbrugh Park front garden</u> anticipates the specimens to be found within.

Entering <u>Greenwich Park</u> is like walking into a kind of landscape museum. The park is on two levels: the southern half is an extension of the Blackheath plateau, the former heathland through which Watling Street runs before it climbs up the wooded slopes of Shooters Hill. This ends in the middle of the park where a steep escarpment quickly lowers the northern half to the level of the riverside plain. The Royal Observatory sits on the brow of the escarpment, from where you can also enjoy the best views of the grand Royal Naval College, the curious Greenwich Power Station, the curving River Thames and the carbuncular mass of Canary Wharf.

51.477113, 0.016664

51.476656, 0.008222

As a Royal Park, Greenwich Park belongs to the crown and
has done since the fifteenth century – public access is only granted
through royal goodwill. Once a deer park, it is enclosed by a wall built
by James I, while the landscaping still in evidence today was devised in
the seventeenth century inspired by plans that the French landscape
architect André Le Nôtre, designer of the gardens at Versailles, drew
up for Charles II. Wandering down the still-intact sweet chestnut-lined
diagonal avenues is fascinating. Many of the original chestnuts
planted 350 years ago survive, supplemented by replanting through
the centuries. As chestnut trees age, their trunks become huge and
gnarled, hollows develop and they often take on a distinct spiral. Each
old tree – once just another identical sapling in a regular avenue – has
developed a unique character. Centuries of climbing, branch removal,
storm damage, lightning strikes and nut gathering have exacted their
toll. Individual trees experience each small event differently and time
amplifies their effects over the years, making neighbouring trees look
quite distinct. Like the Charlton House mulberry, one chestnut, not
in an avenue, has been awarded Great Tree of London status. Secluded
in the <u>Flower Garden</u>, a relatively recent enclosure, its separation may
have resulted in less vigorous management and allowed it to become
even more noble than its parkland siblings.

51.47680I, 0.00691 9

But chestnuts were not the only trees planted back in the 1660s
– elms once defined these avenues, too. Sadly these were lost to Dutch
elm disease, though a few young elms of disease-resistant varieties
have been planted close to the observatory. You can only imagine the
splendours that elm trees would have provided here and elsewhere in
the city, and you have to hope that chestnut blight does not deliver a
second wave of carnage upon this fascinating historic landscape.

The chestnut avenues of Greenwich Park are interspersed with
other trees, including numerous oaks, both evergreen holm and
pedunculate oaks. Blackheath Avenue, the tourist route into the park
from the south, is lined with horse chestnuts. Other landscape enclaves
have also been carved out from the original Restoration-era design.
The inaccessible Wilderness – planned as an area of coppice – provides
a glimpse into the park's Tudor past as a royal hunting ground. Rough
grass surrounds fenced-in trees protected from an elusive deer herd.
A small rose garden on the western side was laid out with radiating beds

in the 1960s, while a children's playground and boating lake adjoin the walled Queen's Orchard in the north-east corner. The orchard has been around since at least 1693 and is the earliest of the park's enclaves. An interesting collection of old fruit tree varieties resides here, including apples, pears, quinces, nectarines and peaches, as well as another old mulberry. The Flower Garden was laid out around a century ago and, despite its name, is most notable for its trees, including a large collection of maturing cedars. Some of London's rare younger cedars of Lebanon grace its well-manicured lawns, representing what may, in 2100, be the finest examples of these trees in the city. Another Great Tree of London is here, too: a towering North American shagbark hickory that produces masses of pecan-like nuts that are eagerly devoured by squirrels. From the mid-nineteenth century onwards, exotic and unusual North American plants were often placed in parks to provide genteel entertainment for a public more conversant in horticulture than they are today. An unusual Kentucky coffeetree harks back to this period – a curiosity as a result of its intriguing name and elegant doubly pinnate, or branched, leaves. Another oddity, this time of a European kind, is a cockscomb beech. A strange slow-growing cultivar of the familiar beech tree, it appears gaunt and ailing from a distance. On close inspection, the reason becomes clear: a mutation has caused the leaves to congregate in tight, deeply incised bunches. This kind of botanical abnormality has, like other cultivars, been perpetuated through grafting, but its limited appeal compared to, say, a copper beech means it is rarely encountered outside large parks or botanical collections.

Admired for centuries – not least by Samuel Pepys, who described it as 'very magnificent' in a diary entry from 1662 – Greenwich Park was the scene of a nineteenth-century environmental battle. London's first steam passenger railway, the London and Greenwich, was opened in the 1830s and plans were mooted for it to continue on a viaduct through the park until intense local opposition saw the plans dropped. We think of nineteenth-century viaducts as part of a distant industrial heritage, but what horror must the residents of Greenwich have felt about something we might now think of as picturesque? How much was the anti-railway campaign about preserving the parkland and how much was it more a nimbyish impulse that, on analysis, we might view as instinctual conservationism?

Compared to the central London Royal Parks, Greenwich is relatively devoid of plane trees, but just beyond the park's western wall, the Regency crescent-cum-square of Gloucester Circus provides the perfect place for plane piners. Within the private central garden you find many fine mature planes and other trees, many hanging over the street of this tightly packed development. One veteran plane is so large that the perimeter fence has been extended to accommodate its girth. Like many older specimens, particularly in squares, it shows signs of historic management regimes – knuckles protrude where limbs branch. But on at least two, if not three occasions, the tree has persuaded its custodians that it should be allowed to soar, so jointed branches have carried the canopy ever higher. It shows no signs of recent pollarding, and every indication that it will continue skywards.

◁ 51.477874, -0.009112

THE ISLE OF DOGS

Pedestrians emerging from the Greenwich Foot Tunnel on the north bank of the Thames are greeted by a small patch of greenery, Island Gardens, home to possibly the Isle of Dogs' first, and certainly its oldest, trees. Old paintings and maps show the 'island' to be a treeless expanse of uninhabited marsh. This was drained in the seventeenth century and the West India Docks were opened in 1802, heralding the area's development into dockland.

◁ 51.486649, -0.009065

Ports have played a key part in shaping London's urban forest for millennia. Since Roman times, and probably before, plants and animals have arrived in the city on boats from overseas: merchants and traders have profited from importing foodstuffs and markets have developed for new and exotic commodities as they have become available. Adventurers have brought back trophies and curiosities from distant lands, while migrants have imported familiar plants and foods to remind them of home. Sweet chestnuts and mulberries arrived with the Romans, while apples and pears may have entered earlier. Potatoes came when the Americas were discovered and thousands more plants, animals and fungi have turned up since. Live plants and animals, fruit and vegetables, grains and seeds have all passed through here, sometimes arriving incognito in shipments of corn or consignments of wool. From these docklands, imports have fanned out in all directions, sometimes not getting far at all. From the seventeenth century, plant hunters would send back new discoveries destined for enlightened collectors in London, while nurseries in Hackney and botanical gardens at Kew or Chelsea might have welcomed later specimens. Exotic animals could be bound for London Zoo, while the Victorian-built Natural History Museum would have been the destination for a plethora of diverse material. And today they keep on coming.

The massive development of the docklands since the late 1980s has resulted in the transformation of a post-industrial wasteland into completely new residential and commercial London neighbourhoods. The most visible of these is Canary Wharf – the end of this trail – where architects and planners, taking their postmodern cues from American cityscapes, have built a city within a city. Softening hard edges and adding grandeur to match the scale of the architecture, trees have been planted since the first new buildings arose from the postwar dereliction. Ironically, perhaps, the Isle of Dogs is now greener and has more trees than it ever did in the past. The urban forest is blossoming here.

Approaching this centrepiece along West India Avenue, large small-leaved limes planted little more than 30 years ago line the boulevard. Elsewhere more limes and planes of the same vintage are doing well. They're rather conservative choices for such a sparkling new development, but perhaps risk-averse planners preferred to opt for tried-and-tested city trees likely to thrive here and that would, through their familiarity, emphasise that this is definitely still London. Elsewhere, developers have been less cautious, and the newly created forest park covering the entrance to Canary Wharf station has been planted with Chinese dawn redwoods. Related to giant redwoods, they are one of the very few deciduous conifers, meaning that they lose their leaves, or needles, each autumn.

The story of the dawn redwood's discovery and subsequent horticultural exploitation is fascinating. During the Second World War, China was at war with Japan and the government, worried the conflict might become protracted, wanted to catalogue the natural resources available in its interior. A surveyor despatched to a remote corner of Hubei province reported a redwood-like tree known locally as 'water fir'. It was not until after the war that other Chinese scientists reached the site of the tree and discovered that not only was it related to American

51.505575, -0.025735

redwoods, but that it was also deciduous and matched fossils of a tree thought to be long since extinct – *Metasequoia glyptostroboides*.

In 1948 seeds from the newly rediscovered tree were sent to arboreta and botanical collections around the world. News of this giant tree that had eluded science for so long made headlines around the world. Seedlings had entered the US horticultural trade by 1951 and it was commercially available here in the UK soon after. With all the publicity surrounding its discovery, dawn redwoods were quickly snapped up and planted in parks, gardens and streets across the US. Since then, it has become a popular constituent of the urban forest in London, and is frequently seen gracing streets around the city, including the A4 in west London. While the wild trees have not been recorded reaching the great heights of American redwoods, they have proven to be fast growing in London, so there's no telling quite how big they might become. One day they may even be knee-high to one of Canary Wharf's skyscrapers.

▲

EPPING
TO
LONDON
FIELDS

▼

EPPING

Arriving at Epping's quiet Victorian <u>tube station</u> on a London Underground train that has rattled through open country beyond the M25 is
a strange experience. Having watched the crammed rush-hour carriage
you boarded at Bank or Bond Street gradually empty of passengers as
it leaves the city, you feel like you're undertaking a journey in time as
well as space. Upon arrival, the rural charms of the town's station seem
to confirm that time is different here at the north-eastern gateway to
Epping Forest. On a map, the forest's outline is considerably longer
than it is wide – it vaguely resembles a mirrored outline of Japan. The
southern half is particularly narrow in places, and there are one or two
detached forest 'islands'. Nevertheless, it's remarkable that such a large
swathe of forest has survived so close to the capital. The City of London
Corporation is the 'conservator' of Epping Forest, which it describes as
'London's largest open space'. In fact, most of the forest lies in Essex,
though it's certainly in the capital's orbit.

    The contemporary meaning of the word 'forest', alien to people
a few hundred years ago, is a large tract of woodland, which accurately
describes the area now approaching. Epping is an ancient forest,
unsettled since the glaciers receded, and supports an intricately linked
ecosystem that has evolved over millennia, with a direct lineage to the
first wildwood. But it is also a forest in the medieval sense – a meaning
that has little to do with trees. The word 'forest' entered the English
language from the Latin word *foris* to mean a place without, or outside
common law, with its own rules and regulations. What's more, Epping

51.693718, 0.113678

is also a dense tract of London's urban forest, part of the city's green infrastructure encompassing everything from the trees and shrubs in its parks, gardens and streets to the woodland within and around its borders. This urban forest directly impacts the city, helping purify its air, moderating its climate and soaking up the rainfall that might otherwise cause flooding. It is a place of resort for city dwellers – for both recreation and for boosting mental and physical wellbeing. We are only just beginning to quantify the value of these less tangible benefits of the urban forest, but we have always known that trees and green spaces make the city more liveable.

BELL COMMON TO AMBRESBURY BANKS

51.690279, 0.097324

Almost the last building in prosperous and unhurried Epping, the Forest Gate Inn, a homely pub on Bell Common heralds the start of the 13 miles and 2,400 hectares of the forest that lie between here and Forest Gate, E7. Just past the pub, the insistent oscillating hum of fast traffic is audible – the sound of the M25 emerging from a too-short tunnel below. Despite the forest's size, traffic noise still seeps into these northern reaches: London's orbital motorway borders the forest for some distance, the M11 is nearby, and other busy local roads cut through it. But calmness is afforded by the enveloping grandeur of the trees and the songs of birds that are, thankfully, much nearer.

Epping's boundaries remain similar to those known in medieval times, but its land use has changed dramatically since. For centuries, it would have looked very different from today's forest. The poor, gravelly soils on the high ground between the Roding and Lea valleys were enough to put off farmers intent on grubbing out the trees. Instead, it became 'wood pasture', an ancient landscape consisting of woods, heaths and grazing land, the latter more or less densely interspersed with trees. It would have been unenclosed, providing sustenance for both domestic animals and wild deer. The monarch had exclusive rights to hunt game throughout the forest and woe betide anyone who interfered with the deer. As one Anglo-Saxon chronicler wrote of William the Conqueror: 'He made large forests for deer and enacted laws therewith, so that whoever killed a hart or a hind should be blinded… he loved the tall stags as if he were their father.'

Numerous gentry and church interests, along with commoners, had rights to graze livestock and harvest wood here. The forest was common land but it had a complex user group with differing rights, so an equally complex system of administration was in place. Medieval forest bureaucracy, with its bye-laws, forest courts and forest officials, may sound unwieldy, but it worked and is the key to why the forest is still here today.

Not far into the woodland, along <u>Forest Road</u> (more a track), you encounter a characterful old hornbeam, providing a taster of what's to come. Sinewy, and fluted with age, its muscular trunk (or 'bolling') is clearly very old. Unlike the former coppice stools found in other ancient London woodlands, this hornbeam has been pollarded at head height. But this has not occurred for some time and, consequently, towering branches have carried the canopy upwards from what would once have been stubby knuckles producing a crop of poles every few years. Further into 'Epping Thicks', as this northern section is known, the legacy of pollarding is evident. Almost every tree is a lapsed pollard, many of them very old.

The old forest system began to break down in the eighteenth and nineteenth centuries when local landlords physically asserted ownership of the open, common land through enclosure. This meant commoners – those living in parishes surrounding the forest – lost their ancient rights to graze and 'lop', or pollard. A campaign against enclosure led by one Thomas Willingale of Loughton eventually won the day – in part. The Epping Forest Act was passed in 1878, ensuring the forest would be protected and public access guaranteed. But while it halted enclosure, it didn't save commoners' lopping rights. The City of London Corporation stepped in to become the new manager of the forest. Consequently, the very last pollarding took place the same year. As pollarding happens on rotation, some trees may not have been lopped since 1860. Since then, the trees, already mature when pollarding ceased, have been left to grow.

Along with hornbeam, there is also oak here but the most numerous, and most dramatic, trees are beech. They have grown into incredible shapes, often resembling inverted elephantine squid with great tentacles sweeping upwards behind bodies buried head-first in the ground. What were once low, rounded trees have risen to create

51.68977, 0.094436

51.68977, 0.087169

a multi-limbed, vaulted forest interior that's dark when the trees are in leaf, and leaden in winter. Silver birch trees have made opportunistic headway into the canopy here and there, while evergreen holly is also common in the Thicks, making the forest darker, spikier and more impenetrable. As in Lesnes Abbey Wood (p55) with its ancient undulations, the ground up here is not level and frequent dips and fleeting, weather dependent streams conspire to disorient. This is a forest to visit with a map and compass: there are few landmarks, little signage and many paths. Phone coverage can be weak or non-existent for long stretches, too.

Beneath the beeches, little grows. It's too dark for most plants, and those that do gain a tenuous foothold will soon be devoured by the deer that still roam here: both fallow and diminutive muntjac can be glimpsed in these quieter parts. The ground is covered with brown leaf litter – slowly rotting leaves from dozens of autumns – interspersed with mosses and, in the farther reaches, the ground feels soft and springy. Is it possible that no other human has walked here for decades? Fallow deer are the same colour as leaf litter, so a quick peripheral movement may be all you perceive of a buck or doe as it flits into the undergrowth.

With a little imagination, the medieval treescape of Epping Forest may still be discerned. The wood pasture landscape that defined the Thicks was woodland grazed less intensely at certain times to allow for tree regeneration – just a couple of decades in a two-century period would do it. The trees would be regularly lopped to put their lowest branches just out of reach of hungry grazers, who instead scratched a living from the woodland floor. Because the trees were kept trim, light could reach the understory, encouraging the growth of more verdant ground plants than the paltry flora of today.

As the forest reaches its highest ground in this area, huge banks appear. Bigger and higher than the boundary-defining woodbanks in the likes of tiny Coldfall Wood (p35), these are the ramparts of the Ambresbury Banks Iron Age hill fort. They're thought to have been constructed 2,500 years ago to provide protective animal enclosures when opposing and sometimes warring tribes clashed. Pollen records show that trees were present at this time, suggesting that the forest was wood pasture for centuries before the medieval period. Ambresbury Banks is an exceptionally eerie place. It's difficult to comprehend its scale in the dense beech forest. Massive banks and ditches carved into the ridge are dotted with ent-like pollards and cloaked in decaying leaves, while people and animals wander through, unaware that the three-metre high banks, over a mile in length, were hand dug by our prehistoric predecessors. This extraordinary and mysterious landscape is a parallel universe.

JACK'S HILL TO GRIMSTON'S OAK

As the path progresses south through Jack's Hill and Great Monk and Little Monk woods, the character of the forest remains consistently deep and dense as another prehistoric earthwork, Loughton Camp, emerges from the gloom. A spot that, more plausibly than Bostall Woods (p58), lays claim to be the location of 'Dick Turpin's Cave', where the notorious highwayman allegedly laid low between robberies. Not far away is the first of several forest highways, Epping New Road, a busy A-road along which significant traffic speeds – perhaps fear of the dense modern forest causes anxious drivers to hit the accelerator. The human psyche seems to harbour a deep-seated fear of untamed forests – maybe we're hardwired to be on our guard from potential predators, both animal and human. Great natural beauty and intangible perils indeed coexist here, though these days the most dangerous parts for both man and beast are surely these roads.

On the western side of Epping New Road, beech starts to succumb to more hornbeam and oak. Pollarding has been initiated by conservationists on the young trees, something the City conservators are funding, even if it is, technically, against their own rules. Most would agree that it's worth maintaining the character of the forest, which should entail some management of the trees. But even with an army of conservation volunteers, it would be impossible to reinstate traditional pollarding across the forest's vast acreage. So is it worth thinking long and hard about re-establishing commoners' lopping rights and allowing freelance cutting? Could Londoners' demands for summer barbecue charcoal be provided by a local and renewable industry? Or has the forest entered a new era in its long history that will see it lose its medieval character and revert to unmanaged woodland?

51.675765, 0.068339

51.658027, 0.050609

When the 1878 Epping Forest Act put paid to active pollarding, it meant the existing heaths became the only long-term grazing land as the ground flora-choking canopy expanded. Victorian legislation saved the forest from destruction, paving the way for today's fantastic environment. But it also ended centuries of historic and sustainable woodland management. Of course, the forest is not set in aspic and the trees will continue to grow and age. Beech and hornbeam are shorter lived than oak, so perhaps future centuries will see the forest's composition change as the new conditions favour different species. It wouldn't be for the first time: pollen records show small-leaved lime once dominated here, though it's now virtually absent. Today many beech trees are beginning to buckle, limbs have sheared off and whole trees have toppled as if their remarkably shallow root plates were on hinges. The rotting hulks of former trees play host to birds, bats and myriad invertebrates, as well as fungi, some so specialist that they are found virtually nowhere else. Whatever is next in store for the forest, these very old dead and dying trees represent an important and rare habitat.

The first open glades occur just south of Cross Roads, another forest highway. As London gets closer, the roads become more frequent and the character of the forest starts to change. Here you find small herds of grazing English Longhorn cattle, an old breed that may also have been seen in centuries past. The rides open up, too, sunlight can penetrate and vegetation is more mixed – brambles, hawthorn, wild crab apple and blackthorn line the way.

Just off the main north-south track, Grimston's Oak is a worthwhile detour. A clearing opens up, allowing you to admire this fine 350-year-old tree. Big and remarkably broad by forest standards and apparently unmolested by Victorian pollarders, it may once have been a marker tree, given that it lies at the junction of several rides.

BUTLER'S RETREAT TO CHINGFORD

Beyond Grimston's Oak, the forest begins to open up into Chingford Plain. More cattle graze here, helping maintain this scrubby grassland, of which wild crab apple is a distinctive component. A rare and intriguing small tree, for many years it was thought to be the wild ancestor of the domestic dessert apple, but DNA studies have shown

51.653364, 0.033405

51.642754, 0.029041

51.636605, 0.020057

this not to be the case. Instead, a familiar bio-migration story of human-aided distribution appears to have played out. Dessert apples originate from the mountains of central Asia, where apple forests can be found to this day. They appear to have been brought west with caravans along the Silk Road in ancient times, reaching Europe thousands of years ago. Travellers may have planted pips as they moved along these routes to provide sustenance for fellow wayfarers in future years, or perhaps to create reminders of home. No doubt, apple munchers would have discarded cores as they progressed, too, further aiding the distribution of apple trees along the ancient highways, just as fruit trees can be spotted lining motorways or railways today. The native wild crab apple, on the other hand, looks quite different. It is often a slight, thorny bush with small leaves producing small and unpalatable yellow fruits. They're good for crab apple jelly, though.

As the plain unfolds, suddenly, it seems, there are buildings. The city has started. As if to ease you in, the first is a quaint old slatted wood building: <u>Butler's Retreat</u>, an old barn converted into a coffee shop. Then next to that is the remarkable <u>Queen Elizabeth's Hunting Lodge</u>, a three storeyed, half-timbered, genuine Tudor building constructed by Elizabeth's father, Henry VIII, as a grandstand from which to view the hunt. Henry had a passion for deer hunting or, rather, watching deer being hunted and had part of the forest enclosed, or imparked, especially for the purpose. This meant the deer were fenced in and the king could enjoy the spectacle of their slaughter from his high-rise 'Great Standing', as the structure was originally known. Elizabeth was also keen on the chase, and while she didn't indulge her passion as much as her father, she did have the building renovated and it was from this time that the current name stuck.

The view from the lodge may be much the same as it was for Henry and Elizabeth – mainly open ground with forest beyond. But emerging above the canopy, eagle-eyed forest spectators may be able to spot what looks like a strangely regular and open tree that most definitely wouldn't have been here in Tudor times. Although masquerading as a giant redwood, this is no tree at all, but rather a not-very-well disguised mobile phone mast. Tree masts come in a variety of styles, none of which stand up to much scrutiny. Resembling comically conspicuous attempts at camouflage, they bring to mind bungling 'Dad's Army' espionage

51.634592, 0.016763 51.633890, 0.017147

ventures and tend to tower over the trees around them – presumably so their signals can pass unhindered. They also seem to take their design inspiration from species absent nearby, in this case a towering conifer. Perhaps those who commission them think no one will notice these pastiche trees or, like the emperor's new clothes, they're just too oblivious to recognise their ridiculousness.

Another edifice rather too near to the lodge is the twentieth-century mock-Tudor building that now houses a Premier Inn. This quaintly familiar architectural style seems dated and reminiscent of middle England, but it was once quite radical. Pioneered in the nineteenth century, Tudorbethan architecture took inspiration from the modest decoration and honest materials used in Tudor buildings and was much in tune with the anti-industrial Arts and Crafts movement and its emphasis on craftsmanship. The style chimed with the growing middle classes, becoming mainstream by the end of the century. Nearby Victoria Road and The Drive typify streets all over London where half timbering has been incorporated into the villas and semis of suburbia. It would be nice to think that the timber used to construct Queen Elizabeth's Hunting Lodge, the Premier Inn and the mock Tudor homes of Chingford was all grown, selected, cut and hauled out of Epping Forest. The lodge's beams and the weatherboards of Butler's Retreat may conceivably have been locally sourced, but those of the more recent buildings almost certainly weren't.

We are now in the London Borough of Waltham Forest. Although the borough was only created in a 1965 local government reorganisation, the name originates from the thirteenth century when it was given to the area of medieval forest jurisdiction encompassing Epping Forest and the now much-depleted Hainault Forest, plus considerably more unwooded land besides. Unlike the patchwork urbanisation found in places such as Barnet and Totteridge, Chingford's suburban streets go head to head with the forest, seemingly ignoring the huge tract of woodland they border. Here you'll find no towering back garden oaks or roundabouts surmounted by beech pollards. Instead these conventional streets are lined with well-maintained hybrid limes and neat, fastigiate hornbeam cultivars. Orderly front gardens are largely green and the scourge of car-friendly concrete is rare. There are planes, too, and a few more exotic species – one street, Gordon Road, is home to unusual Père David's maples from Asia. They're one of the snakebark maples with distinctive green-veined bark that someone must have once thought looked like snakeskin – though certainly not from any Epping Forest serpent.

CHINGFORD TO WOOD STREET

From Chingford Overground terminus, it's just two stops to Wood Street in eastern Walthamstow. The line runs between back gardens with tree-dotted green borders on both sides for much of the journey. This verdant, unvisited edgeland is something of a haven for wildlife and, among the bramble, buddleia, sycamore and ash scrub, foxes idle during summer days. The railway line not only acts as the creatures' daytime hangout, but also their commuter route between town and country.

It's thought there could be over 10,000 foxes in London, a number that has increased significantly in the last decade. The city is clearly much to their liking: an urban forest teeming with food, plenty of shelter and few dangers compared with the countryside. Londoners' relationship with urban foxes must also be a factor in their increasing numbers. Many appear to tolerate them and some positively adore them, even if a few are wary or even scared. Particularly active at dawn and dusk, foxes are often seen brazenly scuttling down central London streets as unconcerned by our presence as we are of theirs – perhaps they equate large numbers of humans with a better, safer environment. But what has changed in the last ten years to precipitate their increased numbers? Might the city's growing population have helped boost the opportunities offered by the urban environment? After all, humans are so messy and wasteful that they often leave food directly on the street or in easy-to-access bags. Foxes (and rats and gulls) must think we positively desire their cohabitation, feeding them and encouraging prey species such as mice and worms – in the latter case by keeping well-tended lawns in the city's less densely populated areas. We're so companionable that we even share our lairs with other canines – something wild foxes must find particularly perplexing. Dogs are frequently rattled by their undomesticated, savage relatives and aggressively seek to see them off their patch. Perhaps a bit of canine ·

Stockholm syndrome has set in with dogs. Desperate to maintain their favoured positions, they rush to protect their jailers from their potentially dangerous wild cousins.

As well as providing safe havens for foxes, railway embankments have developed a distinct flora rich in species from across the world. These young wildernesses represent the ideal conditions for opportunistic plants to thrive and spread. Bindweed, bramble, buddleia, rosebay willowherb and sycamore are, as any commuting plant lover knows, by far the most common species in these spaces, but others are gaining footholds too, including Japanese knotweed, evergreen holm oak, tree of heaven, Russian vine and eucalyptus. Much as the domestic apple spread along ancient caravan routes, railway lines have aided the dispersal of a range of plants. The building and maintenance of lines disturbs the adjacent land, creating a level playing field for new arrivals. Like a landscape born after a natural catastrophe – a volcanic eruption for instance – it's an opportunity for new upstarts to begin consolidating a position unhindered by existing plant communities. The greatest diversity of species tends to be found in more central parts of London and then dissipates out along the train lines. The distinctive tree of heaven – originally from China – with huge frond-like leaves is a common sight in the centre of town, but as the railways radiate further out, it becomes increasingly infrequent, virtually disappearing as tracks hit the home counties.

WALTHAMSTOW

Wood Street station may be just a few minutes on the train from the more sedate Chingford, but it could be a world away. This is proudly Walthamstow and it's a place on the up, fizzing with self-confidence as London's relentless wave of gentrification ripples eastwards. Separated from much of the city by the marshes of the Lea Valley on its western border, Walthamstow has developed apart and has a distinct feel about it. Civic pride finds expression in the palatial Scandi-modernist town hall set in extensive manicured grounds with a still-functioning fountain (how many London town halls can boast one of those?) and flowerbeds featuring kaleidoscopic begonias, petunias and canna lilies.

51.590792, -0.013430

Heading north out of Wood Street station, a large tree comes into view down the road. This is the Wood Street horse chestnut, a Great Tree of London. It towers over a single-storey, late eighteenth-century weatherboarded building, once the local butcher and now, somewhat ironically, an organic whole foods shop. The tree must be getting on for 200 years old (a grand old age for a horse chestnut) and now dominates this corner of Walthamstow. Familiar to many for their flower candles, large palmate leaves and autumnal crop of conkers, horse chestnuts are sadly another tree in trouble. By high summer, many are already looking like autumn has arrived as their foliage turns brown and starts to wither. This forlorn appearance is caused by swarms of minute caterpillars – leaf miners – eating their way through the insides of the leaves. These ravenous grubs and their parent moths were unknown before they were first recorded in the horse chestnut homeland of northern Greece in the 1980s and have spread far and wide since, arriving in Wimbledon in 2002. But affected trees continue to put out new leaves and flowers every spring, followed by abundant chestnuts in the autumn, so, beyond making them look unsightly, the leaf miners don't seem to be causing too many problems. That said, munching away year after year, they must be reducing the trees' ability to photosynthesise and may induce long-term stress. One other less obvious problem on the increase is canker, a debilitating condition causing sap to bleed out of open wounds. It's possible it could be taking advantage of trees weakened by leaf miner activity.

Further down Wood Street, several striking trees hang over the pavement from the playground of Woodside Academy primary school. There's a golden-leaved false acacia in the middle, perhaps the most head-turning yellow foliaged tree around. It's flanked by two other trees that, at certain times of year, might be mistaken for the same species. Both have large, roundish, heart-shaped leaves up to 30 centimetres long but, look closely, and their completely different seed pods will confirm that they are unrelated. One has upward-pointing bunches of what look like small round nuts that persist through the winter. This is a foxglove or princess tree, which in late April or early May of some years produces a stunning show of blue trumpet-like flowers and is pretty much the only, and certainly the most common, large, blue-flowered tree seen in London. Meanwhile, its lookalike companion

51.589214, -0.004430

51.590784, -0.004472

has the long dangling seeds of an Indian bean tree from the US Deep South. These distinctive bean-like pods remain on the tree in winter and demand revisiting in July when the tree comes into blousy flower with large horse chestnut-like flower spikes. Both trees also share a fast growth rate, reaching maturity in a few decades and, in the case of the Indian bean tree, enter recumbent old-age at a mere 150 years.

Turning the corner, and heading west on Forest Road, brown signs point to the William Morris Gallery. A writer, designer, printer, socialist activist and leading light of the Victorian Arts and Crafts movement, Morris looms large over Walthamstow. The gallery on Forest Road is accommodated in a fine <u>Georgian house</u>, formerly 'Water House', the Morris family's country home from 1848 to 1856. The Arts and Crafts movement found popular expression through Morris's textile designs, which combined organic, folk and medieval motifs. Morris's earlier childhood was spent in nearby Woodford Hall (now demolished) with 50 acres of grounds adjoining Epping Forest. As a precocious and privileged child – who had his own suit of armour and a pony – the young William would play in the forest, where he got to know the woodland plants and animals, and developed a particular fascination for the ancient earthworks of Loughton Camp and Ambresbury Banks. At the time of Morris's childhood explorations, Epping Forest would still have been managed traditionally, and would have differed considerably from today's dark, empty and, in places, eerie forest. Certainly the regularly managed pollards would have been much more open, more light would have penetrated to the forest floor and the undergrowth would have been more abundant. This natural playground surely made an impression on Morris, whose enduring fabric designs employ a range of natural plant and animal designs. While some were given specific names such as 'Bird and Anemone', 'Tulip' or 'Iris', they portray stylised, unspecific images in a way that recalls memories or feelings of bosky, rural idylls.

Epping Forest would also have been a much busier place when young William first knew it. Traditional woodland enterprises, little altered for 600 years and in tune with the seasons and rhythms of nature, would be commonplace. Local parishioners would still be exercising their ancient rights to graze livestock and collect firewood, and various craftspeople would have been found carrying out their time-honoured work. At different times of year, you would have

51.59091, -0.020605

encountered everyone from woodsmen cutting fuel destined for London's fireplaces and highly skilled hurdle-makers crafting fence panels from newly lopped poles, to faggot-makers bundling brushwood and charcoal-producers with their elaborate smouldering fire mounds. The continuity of craft traditions and skills handed down through generations, and the harmonious, non-destructive nature of woodland work appears to have informed the adult, socialist Morris. In his 1884 lecture 'Art and Socialism', he said that 'Nothing should be made by man's labour which is not worth making; or which must be made by labour degrading to the makers.' This philosophy, which may in part have been derived from his experiences of Epping Forest, informed his company Morris & Co's approach to manufacturing textiles, tiles and other products. It is a testament to the inspiration of nature and a commitment to traditional craft skills that Morris's designs still deck the halls of countless homes and public buildings throughout the city and far beyond.

The former garden of Water House, complete with its moated square island, is now part of Lloyd Park, the largest surviving open space in Walthamstow and home to some of the biggest and oldest trees in E17. Walthamstow used to be a village centred on its church with several outlying houses and farms in open fields stretching from the edge of Epping Forest to the River Lea. The current dense suburb was laid out after the arrival of the railways in the late nineteenth century, but the grounds of Water House and its seventeenth-century moat were preserved. Parallel to Forest Road, well-groomed Winns Avenue runs west from Lloyd Park towards the Lea. A street of brick terraces, nearly all behind privet hedges, it is a consistent boulevard lined with striking birch trees, most of the same age, which adds to its appeal. Two species have been selected for the job: some are North American paper birch, but most are Asian Himalayan birch. The latter has the whitest bark of all the birches, more so even than the silver birch. From the turn of the millennium, they have been one of the most frequently planted trees in London – in contrast to their status in their native Nepal and Kashmir, where pressure on land is leading to deforestation and impacting their future. It would be grimly ironic if these dazzling birches were to become more frequent on the streets of London than growing wild in the high Himalayas.

51.592319, -0.020986

51.592130, -0.025373

WALTHAMSTOW WETLANDS TO WICK WOODLAND

Where the broad Lea valley floodplain opens up marks the edge of Walthamstow. Forest Road continues through this landscape of sky, plain and water, first crossing the River Lea Flood Relief Channel, a sorry-looking waterway encased in concrete, then extending past reservoirs punctuated by willows on the north and south. It then crosses the Coppermill Stream and reaches the Ferry Boat Inn before bridging the River Lea proper. Opposite this quaint old pub is the entrance to the southern part of Walthamstow Wetlands, a 211-hectare nature reserve enclosing several reservoirs still supplying water to Londoners. It's a tranquil place and, from the viewing area at the renovated Engine House, it's possible to comprehend the Lea Valley south to the gleaming towers of the City and Docklands. The Lea is London's second river, and its impact on the landscape is significant. Effectively splitting the East End in half, the broad, formerly marshy Lea valley (or 'Lee' to some), with its mesh of waterways, stretches from Ware in Hertfordshire to the Thames, with relatively little urban development along its course. As a non-urban, watery wedge through the city, it acts as a navigational aid for migrating birds, and the reservoirs at Walthamstow attract huge numbers of waterfowl, particularly in winter. As a result, they are famed internationally for gadwalls, shovelers and tufted ducks, the first two in flocks so big that this is one of the best sites for them in Europe. There are always lots of other birds to be seen throughout the year, too. An island in one reservoir is home to London's largest heronry, where dozens of large and charismatic grey herons nest. Elegant white egrets, actually a kind of small heron, also breed here, while the very lucky might catch sight of a jewel-like kingfisher. It is astonishing to think that London hosts internationally important bird colonies, but it proves both how adaptable nature can be and how well cities and wildlife can coexist.

Between the reservoirs, footpaths pick their way through the willow- and alder-bounded causeways leading eventually to the reserve's southern exit on to hedge-fringed Coppermill Lane. The lane peters out at a car park used, in the daytime at least, by dog walkers, but continues as a pedestrian route under the Liverpool Street–Stansted railway line and, beyond a discreet gate, into another nature reserve: Walthamstow Marshes. With a bit of imagination these empty grasslands are reminiscent of a Dutch landscape painting. A flat expanse of immense skies bordered by waterways dotted with trees, it feels remote and windswept here, though a glimpse of the electricity pylons and railway lines are generally enough to remind romantically minded visitors that they're still in twenty-first century London. Even so, the fields are abuzz with insects in the summer: rare Essex skipper butterflies flit around the grassland, restless dragonflies dart chaotically, and a variety of marshland birds, including willow and sedge warblers, can all be seen. The scrub, kept in check by grazing cattle, is dominated by brambles and sallow, or goat willow, a broad-leaved small tree with few distinguishing features except in early spring when its conspicuous, fluffy catkins give rise to its other name of pussy willow.

The Capital Ring Walk follows the western edge of the marshes from here to Hackney and beyond. As the river bends and emerges from under the Lea Bridge Road, a path heads east to yet another nature reserve. On the peninsula between the old Lea and the 'Hackney Cut' artificial channel lies the former Middlesex Filter Beds, a Victorian water treatment plant that, like the nearby Essex Filter Beds (now the WaterWorks Centre), closed down 50 years ago. Since then the sites have more or less been left to their own devices. The WaterWorks Centre Nature Reserve has been managed to appeal to birdwatchers with each of its former filter beds offering slightly different environments to attract a wide range of species. A glamorous hoopoe even called in here once. The Middlesex Filter Beds have been less managed and illustrate how nature moves in once human activity stops. Five decades ago this was an industrial site – water from the reservoirs upstream was filtered through gravel-filled pools, or beds, to remove impurities before being pumped to homes. When the beds were decommissioned, they were drained and the gravel removed. Gradually nature encroached: first willow and poplar took hold, accompanied by hawthorn and elder. Some of these pioneer willows are now enormous and beginning to split apart. In their wake, and as the soil becomes fixed, other species are starting to dip a toe in. Ash and sycamore are frequent and, in places, holm oak is being cut back. Occasional birch, oak and horse chestnut saplings are also popping up. Through this tangle of woodland, the original Victorian walls, granite-paved surfaces and the remains of old machinery still stand. Given what nature has achieved in just 50 years, the reserve's resemblance to an Indiana Jones-style lost temple is only going to increase in the future.

Another species found on the banks of the Lea around these parts is charismatic giant hogweed. It's easy to spot. An umbellifer, it resembles gargantuan cow parsley, sometimes standing five metres tall and has midsummer flower heads up to 80 centimetres across. Signs hereabouts warn against approaching this much-maligned triffid whose sap sensitises human skin to sunlight, leading to blistering and rashes. But we seem to forget that it was humans who brought this curiosity to London from its home in the Caucasus and central Asia. Victorian gardeners were huge fans, planting it everywhere, but the plant soon developed itchy feet and, according to many, made its original escape from Buckingham Palace. Like water-borne buddleia, giant hogweed has used rivers and canals to aid its migration throughout the UK, but unlike buddleia, it hasn't got much further than the disturbed banks of watercourses, which tend to be mostly urban and consequently visible. There's been a lot of commotion about the perceived dangers of giant hogweed and an industry exists to remove it along with several other plants officially known as 'noxious weeds' (including Japanese knotweed). Also spoken of as an 'undesirable alien' invading our river-banks and shading out native plants, it's even an offence to plant or dispose of it. But such hysteria could be misplaced. Several naturalists refute the shading-out charge, saying it only takes hold where the ground is disturbed and that while it can cause painful skin reactions, so do stinging nettles. Perhaps we need to take a more enlightened view of how we think about giant hogweed and similar plants. Certainly we should educate people about the harm it can cause, but demonising it seems unjust. After all, at one time we thought it fascinating and attractive, and worthy of planting in royal herbaceous borders.

At Hackney, the marshes have been subject to more development. In the aftermath of the Second World War, they were used for dumping debris from the Blitz as London began to rebuild. Now they're a landscape of endless football pitches screened by mature alders, willows, poplars and other water-loving species. On the westward side, as the Capital Ring path emerges from under the

Homerton Road bridge, an unexpected patch of trees appears. This is
Wick Woodland. Before it became a wood, it was an unloved piece of
amenity grassland across the road from the Hackney Marshes. Then,
in the mid 1990s, the A12 between Hackney Wick and the M11 was
constructed, one of the last large-scale destructive road schemes to go
ahead in London. Protests centred on a 250-year-old sweet chestnut
on George Green in Wanstead. It was eventually destroyed along with
more than 200 houses that lay in the expressway's path. As 'mitigation'
for the new road's environmental impact, the former grassland was
planted with trees in the winter of 1996/7.

In little more than 20 years, the wood has blossomed. Despite
traffic thundering along the A12 on its southern border, this is a remarkably
tranquil place. For the last ten years it has been managed by local
volunteers, the 'Tree Musketeers', and feels like a woodland that is
loved and valued by many. But it's also a well-used space and keeping
it clear of rubbish must be a never-ending task. Empty cans, bottles and
small metal nitrous oxide capsules are dotted about and, close to the
A12, plastic packaging and other jettisoned detritus is frequent. But, like
the Middlesex Filter Beds, Wick Woodlands shows how rapidly trees
and wildlife can take over. Growth rates here are helped by the fact that
the trees are planted on the rich soil of a floodplain. Most of today's
ancient woodlands sit on poor soils – the main reason they've survived
is because their sites were of little use for agriculture. These woodlands
were originally planted with fast-growing poplar, willow and birch,
which provided a good screen for the other trees that are now taking
hold, which include field maple, ash and yew. Coppicing has started
here too: hazel stools have been cut, and the resulting poles used either
at the nearby Hackney Community Tree Nursery, or to construct dead
hedges to attract other wildlife. Hedgehogs have been recorded and
plants such as wood anemone have also arrived. Sycamore is noticeable
by its absence – according to one original planter, it has, remarkably, yet
to arrive – but some exotic species are present, including a fine avenue
of planes marking the border with the river. A couple of young giant
redwoods lurk in the depths, too.

HOMERTON TO LONDON FIELDS

Hackney has seen a rapid change in its fortunes since the late 1990s. It was once a byword for urban deprivation and, while it cannot claim to have solved all its problems, its closeness to the City and better transport links since the arrival of the London Overground has seen it become a desirable area in which to live, work and play. To those who know it well, it may be no surprise to learn that Hackney is also to be noted as an unofficial urban arboretum. For many years, greening the streets of the borough was, understandably, a low priority and as a result relatively few street trees were planted here compared with more affluent boroughs, such as neighbouring Islington and nearby Camden. But all that started to change 20 years ago.

Now, there are over 300 different street tree species and cultivars in Hackney. As elsewhere in London, some of these are old and characterful planes, but on the less grand thoroughfares, an astonishing diversity of rare and exotic species can be found that, like the borough's residents, originate from all corners of the globe. Hackney's trees are, on the whole, young like its human population, too.

Opposite Homerton station on Berger Road, a pair of pagoda trees welcome new arrivals. Just past them, there's a golden rain tree and, not far away, a pair of variegated American sweetgums mark the turn into Steven's Avenue from Morning Lane. These are unusual street trees, and are just a taster of what lies ahead on a route across the borough to London Fields station. Meandering down to the corner of Brenthouse Street and Elsdale Road, recently planted trees emerge out of the pavement protected by wrought-iron tree guards. Metal cages are essential for keeping trees safe in the inner city and a far cry from the ineffective wooden stakes of old – one Hackney-based Young British Artist, Keith Coventry, made a series of bronzes cast from vandalised saplings complete with stakes in the 1990s. Not only do the more secure metal guards protect trees from all but the most determined tree-snappers, but they also defend against another menace: powerfully jawed dogs. Ten-year-old tree trunks represent ideal jaw-strengthening equipment, and in places where tree guards are not used, young trees often suffer from mauled boles. The new trees on this corner include a rare Chang's sweetgum from Taiwan, one of only a handful in London

– probably half of which are located in Hackney. The related American sweetgum, also present on this corner, is much more common and an increasingly planted species, but it can confuse. It has palmately lobed leaves similar to a maple or a plane, but its fruits are woody balls. This helps distinguish it from maples, which hold their fruits in pairs of winged samara, but, misleadingly, planes have balls, too. So, to be absolutely sure, a resolute sweetgum identifier must wait for late autumn when the leaves will often turn bright crimson.

Heading south-east, the next turning off Elsdale Road is Loddiges Road and it's marked by an unusual hybrid Lucombe oak – a cross between a cork oak and a Turkey oak that originally occurred in the garden of eighteenth-century nurseryman William Lucombe in Exeter. The name of the street pays homage to a dynasty of German émigré horticulturalists. The Loddiges (rhymes with 'bridges') were the founders of the Hackney Botanic Nursery Garden, which occupied the site of the present-day town hall and included what was, in 1816, the world's largest hothouse. Joachim Loddiges started the business in 1777 as global exploration and trade were taking off and Enlightenment hunger for scientific knowledge was at its peak. Through his contacts with plant collectors around the world, he began obtaining seeds and selling them on to wealthy clients from European estates and botanical gardens. Soon, the family firm was growing plants, too, and over several generations it was responsible for introducing thousands of new species, including rhododendrons, camellias, bamboos and, most notably, wisteria. By the 1860s, Hackney, a country village when Joachim arrived, was fast becoming a populous London suburb with rising land prices and the Loddiges were forced to sell up in the face of the unstoppable urban expansion. Their legacy, though, lives on. Loddiges supplied plants to parks and gardens across London and far beyond. Kew was a client, as was nearby Abney Park cemetery in Stoke Newington where several rare trees from the Hackney nursery are still going strong, including a spotted thorn and a western catalpa.

The Loddiges' story is one of migrant success, global trade and scientific curiosity. Their impact on the urban forest of today is significant and, of all the plants they introduced, perhaps two species have defined their legacy. The first is *Rhododendron ponticum*, the common rhododendron, an attractive evergreen shrub with mauve flowers now considered

51.543225, -0.049377

51.545056, -0.056066

invasive with many landowners cursing the day it was introduced. The other is *Wisteria sinensis*, the much-loved climbing wisteria. With its beautiful bunches of pastel blue flowers in spring, who could imagine a stuccoed London terrace without it? It is fitting that a Hackney street – even one lacking in Georgian architectural eye candy – has been named after the family. It's also appropriate that their former Hackney home is the London borough pioneering the planting of such a wide variety of street trees, many of them taking root in the city for the first time.

Hackney's street tree population is interesting not only because it encompasses such a fascinating array of trees, but also as an exercise in strategic planting. London's signature plane trees are found all over the city, but today these represent just two to three per cent of its street trees compared with around 60 per cent a century ago. This figure does not mean we have lost trees; it merely reflects how the urban forest has grown and become more diverse over the years. Last century saw one of history's most significant arboreal catastrophes play out: Dutch elm disease wiped out an estimated 25 million trees across the UK. London had a relatively small elm population, and was not so badly hit, but the trauma of this disease is still felt today. In North America, some cities were planted as elm monocultures with block after block of American elms. Like English elms, these were susceptible to the disease and vast numbers were destroyed. With sad irony, many of them had been planted to replace American chestnuts wiped out by chestnut blight. Worse still, American cities are now dealing with another devastating tree pest: emerald ash borer, a beetle that devastates ash trees, which in some places were planted to replace the elms. The North American experience of tree pests and diseases has led urban foresters to increasingly plant a more diverse array of species to reduce the impact of any future attack. The logic is that if one species succumbs to disease, the overall effect on a street or city will be less. London has been spared the devastation of these American plagues, but as problems with trees such as horse chestnut, ash, sweet chestnut and plane mount up, it is, surely but sadly, only a matter of time. In this light, Hackney's policy of street tree diversity makes perfect sense.

Hackney's enthusiastic planting makes sense in terms of climate, too. The inner city is subject to the urban heat island effect: plaster, brick, concrete, glass and steel soak up heat during the day and release it at night. Temperatures are as much as 10°C higher in the capital compared with the surrounding countryside. This warmer environment, coupled with the impermeable surfaces of city streets, mean trees have to cope with a climate that is hotter and drier than that of, say, adjacent Essex or Surrey. Thus the species best suited to these urban conditions are, unsurprisingly, not always the trees of the English countryside. On the streets of Hackney, olives, figs, peaches and persimmons ripen, and one borough tree officer is convinced that lemons would thrive here, too.

As Loddiges Road approaches Mare Street, several unusual European hop hornbeams stand and, on Mare Street, the central reservation of Hackney's main thoroughfare has been planted with dawn redwoods. If they survive in this exposed position, they will be an impressive sight in years to come. London Lane off Mare Street's western side hosts a row of oriental planes, which judging by their size were installed before the main planting endeavour. These are one of the parent species of the hybrid London Plane. Gransden Avenue, a turning off London Lane, is home to a Japanese lilac, a variegated box elder, and two or three hibiscus trees.

There's also an intriguing tree here without an English name. This may be because it's only been around for a few decades. Or it could be because it comes from Uzbekistan or because it's a hybrid. Whatever the case, its Latin name is × *Chitalpa tashkentensis*. The '×' at the start denotes hybridity, in this case between two North American species – desert willow, *Chilopsis linearis*, and western catalpa, *Catalpa speciosa* – but because these are trees from different genera, the '×' appears at the start. Bizarrely, and not a little ironically given the backdrop of the Cold War, the hybrid was developed in Tashkent, then in the Soviet Union, now in Uzbekistan, hence the '*tashkentensis*' part of the name. So what was the point? Well, not only is × *Chitalpa* able to cope with the drought and heat of a central Asian summer, it's also very frost tolerant and it produces late season flowers when few other trees are blooming. It seems to do OK in London, but would probably prefer hotter, drier summers. There's another on Sidworth Street just round the corner, which is flanked by an unruly tamarisk – not likely to last long – and an Australian bottlebrush tree.

51.5424665, -0.0552206

51.541933, -0.056670

51.541377, -0.056779

Turning the corner into <u>Mentmore Terrace</u>, more exotic Asian species stand out. There's a couple of peanut butter trees, or glorybowers, which promise to be great small street trees that will no doubt be frequently planted beyond Hackney in the future. It has wonderfully fragrant white flowers in July followed by bizarre-looking purple berries surrounded by red star-shaped, cushion-like growths. Despite these features, it owes its peanut-butter name to the fragrance of its crushed leaves.

Opposite the entrance to London Fields station, where this trail ends, there's another unusual tree: a bee-bee tree or euodia from Korea. There are others in Hackney, too, but usually this species is only seen in specialist collections, such as Kew Gardens. Only a few decades ago, it would have been difficult to imagine that Hackney would be blazing a trail for city trees, but what has happened here represents part of the future of the urban forest. In years to come, diverse street tree planting will become the norm in London. It will be worth remembering the experiment started in Hackney.

RICHMOND
PARK
TO
WESTMINSTER

KINGSTON GATE TO RICHMOND GATE

Approaching Richmond Park from Kingston, there is little hint of what lies ahead. In this extremity of suburban London, the park has been completely hidden behind the gardens of the Victorian villas that back right on to it. Busy Queen's Road, the shortest route to well-heeled Richmond, ploughs straight through, breaching the perimeter with little ceremony – just a couple of cast-iron gateposts are squeezed in between leafy front gardens, while a somewhat perfunctory road sign announces 'Kingston Gate, Richmond Park, National Nature Reserve'. As Richmond is a deer park, the gates are shut after dark to keep deer in and traffic out.

At 955 hectares, Richmond Park is big: the largest of London's Royal Parks and the biggest enclosed space in London. Many, sometimes competing, interests are carefully balanced here: the historic cultural landscape, the important plant and animal communities, and various subcategories of human visitors, including motorists. Might driverless cars one day be hard-coded to take the long way round?

Past the gate, the defining feature of this complex corner of the urban forest soon becomes apparent: open, deer-cropped parkland. Great drifts of coarse blond grass and increasing seas of bracken flow over the park's gentle contours, opening up a series of almost primeval vistas. Aged trees and patches of woodland stop it becoming desolate steppe and it is made magical when even just one of its 650-odd deer – red and fallow in roughly equal numbers – wander into view. Their impact on the park is considerable. For centuries, deer have kept the parkland trim and continue to maintain its character. No young trees or seedlings can escape their voracious gorging, and a neat sight-line of around 120 centimetres is maintained under mature tree canopies – the furthest reach of a red deer's tongue.

Among the thousands of trees, a large number – around 1,300 – are ancient and veteran. These are trees that are either getting beyond maturity or so old that they are obviously in decline. The majority are oaks, but there are also old sweet chestnuts and hawthorns. Most of the oaks have been pollarded in the distant past, giving rise to their memorable squat appearance. But unlike the tightly packed pollards of Epping Forest that are maximised for wood production, here the focus has always been on raising and sustaining deer, so trees are fewer and further between. With all that space, many specimens are broader than they are high and some are older than the park itself, having previously formed part of the network of commons and hedgerows that existed here before. You'll find the highest concentration of the oldest and most characterful trees in the Kingston Gate corner. High Wood, just next to Isabella Plantation, is home to dozens of great, fat oaks and represents one of the most important sites anywhere for old English, or pedun-culate oaks. These corpulent trees are important for their cultural and aesthetic value (which for many is enough), but also for their scientific interest to ecologists and naturalists. One of two oak species native to London, pedunculate oaks have acorns on 'peduncles' or stalks, and stalkless leaves. This is reversed in the other less common native, the very similar sessile oak, which has stalkless acorns and leaves with stalks. Both species play a key role in our diverse ecosystem, hosting many more associated species than other trees. As they get older, the guest list grows. Oak trees are very long lived – some can reach 800 years – and have a very long senescent stage: if they mature at 200, they might reach old age at 300, and be in decline and start collapsing over the next 400 or 500 years. Richmond Park is littered with broken and twisted oak limbs left where they fell to gently decompose over decades. Old trees develop hollows that make ideal homes for foxes, bats and other creatures and their decrepitude is aided by a whole ecosystem of insects and fungi that specialise in taking advantage of these arboreal pensioners. Sturdy bracket fungi such as chicken of the woods or beefsteak are common, along with much rarer types that specialise in breaking down

51.43140, -0.28119

dead wood in very old trees. Insects abound, too: this is the heartland of harmless but alarming stag beetles, and is also important for other unusual insects that make their homes among the detritus of decaying trees. Stag beetle larvae will live in decomposing wood for up to five years before emerging as great, antlered beasts in early summer, hence the importance of leaving fallen branches where they lie.

Astonishingly, then, south-west London is home to a world-class nature reserve that represents a type of environment found in few other places in the world. Richmond Park contains more ancient oak trees than you'll find in the whole of some European countries. It's also larger and younger than many other deer parks, most of which have medieval origins: it was only enclosed by Charles I in 1637. Perhaps because of its proximity to the seats of power, the River Thames (the quickest route through London for many centuries), and its popularity with subsequent royals, it has survived largely intact. Deer parks differ from forests, woodlands and chases by the fact that they have been 'imparked', or fenced off, from land that may have had other uses. Such spaces were likely to be either already royal lands or imparked by royal decree and were often bestowed on favoured nobles and managed as game-hunting estates. From the Norman conquest onwards – perhaps even before – venison was considered a food for kings and, consequently, deer were the property of the crown. Deer parks were thus exclusively the gift of monarchs and became sought-after status symbols for ambitious aristocrats.

Beyond High Wood, the forest garden of Isabella Plantation beckons. Fenced off from hungry deer, it makes it immediately clear how different the park would look without their insatiable appetite for all things green. Rather than inspired by some Caroline lover or Georgian princess, the plantation's romantic-sounding name is thought to be a corruption of 'isabel', an archaic word for 'dingy' or 'greyish-yellow' – a reference to its poor sandy soils. Nevertheless, that dreary earth has propagated an enchanted glade that's especially wonderful in May when, wandering north from the plantation's High Wood Gate, masses of azaleas and ornamental rhododendrons, planted around ponds and streams, erupt into a bewitching display of white, reds, purples and every shade in between. As spring progresses and the tree canopy comprising dozens of different species comes into leaf,

51.433780, -0.276782

it starts to resemble some kind of lush temperate rainforest. This notion is compounded by the incessant screeching of ring-necked parakeets, the most conspicuous bird in the plantation and, indeed, the wider park.

Emerging from Isabella Plantation at Peg's Pond Gate, parkland again dominates before eventually giving way to enclosed woodland. Queen Elizabeth's Plantation, along with its northern neighbour, Sidmouth Wood, is a tract barred to deer, dogs and humans. As a result, rhododendrons thrive here, but these are mauve common rhododendron, the first species from this genus introduced to London from southern Europe by Loddiges of Hackney (p93). The species is now regarded as invasive not only here but in many other woods and heaths where it thrives on poor acid soils. Its evergreen foliage shades out virtually every other competing plant and removing it is a huge undertaking, but measures are now underway to control it here.

The two woods are divided by a strip of unenclosed trees, and it's among these, on the eastern side, where one of Richmond Park's great treasures lies: the Royal Oak. This is the park's ancient oak benchmark with a bloated, fissured trunk exposing a great, dark hollow. Only as high as a house, it was once pollarded above the deer line, and over the centuries, what was once a mass of poles have settled into an unruly domed crown composed of a dozen or so twisted limbs. Like the mulberries of south-east London (p57), this tree is now surrounded by a protective fence. But despite the fact that it is one of the Great Trees of London, there is no interpretive signage and it isn't marked on the official maps. It is unclear why it is known as the Royal Oak beyond the obvious explanation (that it stands in a Royal Park) and experts disagree about its age, with estimates ranging from between 550 and 750 years. Because it's hollow, a postmortem ring count will not serve to enlighten us and, anyway, when its time eventually does come, it should surely be left to slowly moulder as a home for future generations of stag beetles.

Following the perimeter of Sidmouth Wood, a sign attached to a locked gate announces that this is a 'Wildlife Sanctuary'. Within, a ride cuts straight through the trees and across the sight line from nearby King Henry's Mound, which offers a 'protected view' to St Paul's Cathedral. This and other officially protected views have determined planning decisions across London, particularly in the

51.44350, -0.28240

51.44447, -0.28544

51.44463, -0.28351

51.44494, -0.29480

City, where skyscraper outlines have been angled to accommodate a view of the cathedral. From the Mound, the vista is framed by trees and the gleaming white dome of St Paul's is visible ten miles away (although some claim that this has been ruined by the construction of a Stratford tower block several miles further east). From the less theatrical Sidmouth Wood spot, you get a panoramic view to St Paul's flanked by the Barbican towers to its north and the silhouettes of the City's skyscrapers – a particularly curious outline from here – plus the outlying Shard to the south. To the south-east and far nearer, you can spot a row of regular modernist slab blocks – the large and much-admired Alton Estate in Roehampton, a postwar housing development incorporating utopian architectural principles. Like the Barbican estate (p46), it was created in a moment of optimism, providing high-quality social housing set within extensive landscaped grounds, and enviable views over Richmond Park for many residents, too.

Continuing around the wood, the path follows Sawyer's Hill, one of the roads leading to the Georgian Richmond Gate and out to Richmond proper beyond. The roads running through the park may appear anachronistic to some visitors, but they nevertheless allow the occupants of cars to experience this remarkable landscape. They also confirm public access rights, which have been cherished for centuries with only brief interruptions. Park users – in cars, on foot or on two wheels – along with the residents of the Alton Estate and other parkside addresses, are the space's unofficial guardians, bearing witness, expressing opinions and cherishing it. Through watching and experiencing the park, they will ensure its continuity.

51.44874, -0.28758

RICHMOND HILL TO ASGILL HOUSE

Despite its distance from the centre of London, Richmond feels cosmopolitan. It maintains a distinct character of its own, and is definitely not suburban. Situated at the end of the District Line, it looks confidently away from the metropolis, peering over the precipice of Richmond Hill to the arcadian provinces beyond.

51.45240, -0.29883

One of the best viewpoints from Richmond Hill is opposite the Roebuck pub – which ironically references a deer species absent from Richmond Park – where the trees part above the precipitous Terrace to afford a sweeping view of the upper Thames valley beyond. This sublime prospect, famously captured on multiple occasions by Joshua Reynolds and, later, JMW Turner, has changed little over the past two centuries. The Terrace descends to Petersham Meadows in turn giving way to Ham House. But it is the wooded Glover's Island sitting mid-Thames with Marble Hill beyond that defines the view to the south-west. In the far distance, a few church spires, omnipresent cranes, and one or two tall buildings are all that poke above the otherwise continuous tree canopy. But surely this is an optical illusion. A swathe of London, encompassing whole suburbs and transport systems, lies hidden in this forest. As the constant stream of low-flying aircraft reminds you – one every two minutes when the flightpath is overhead – Heathrow is only a couple of miles to the west.

The zig-zag down to the riverside through the Terrace passes many fine trees – several cedars, a couple of large ginkgoes and a big oriental plane – but one of the most interesting, midway down the slope, is quite easily overlooked. It is a relatively small, but very unusual true service tree. Related to other *Sorbus* species such as rowan, whitebeam and wild service, true service is closest to rowan in leaf shape, but altogether more substantial – and longer-lived. Rare, and with a primarily southern continental range extending as far north as Brittany, it has always fascinated those with a sensitivity for trees. People have willed true service trees to grow in Britain for a long time. Famously, in 1678 a single tree known as the Whitty Pear was recorded thriving in the Wyre Forest of the Shropshire and Worcestershire borders. Its descendants have continued to grow there and, with great excitement, in recent years small native populations have been found on inaccessible cliffs in south Wales and Gloucestershire. They bear small edible apple- or pear-shaped fruits, but the trees are so scarce throughout their range that recipes for these rare fruits must only exist in folk memory. What makes them so intriguing? Perhaps it's a combination of their curious name, their rarity and the edibleness of their fruits, which offer potential for a whole new flavour. As well as this Richmond tree, several mature, fruit-bearing examples – locally celebrated – grace the grounds of St Ann's Hospital near Green Lanes in Haringey, and Clapton Square in Hackney hosts a pair, too.

A Georgian grotto-subway under the Petersham Road emerges by an enormous London plane on the Thames side in Buccleuch

51.45162, -0.30178

51.45284, -0.29994

51.45311, -0.30240

Gardens. With an on-demand water source and rich alluvial soils to grow in, trees do well along these riverbanks. Heading downstream towards Richmond Bridge particularly large planes are stationed at regular points all along the embankment. One that demands special admiration rises from the terrace of a riverside restaurant. Perhaps 200 years old, the Richmond Riverside Plane is a marvel of natural structural engineering and is another Great Tree of London. Huge limbs are held aloft effortlessly by a trunk that continues to reach skywards and shows no signs of slowing down. Continuing through Richmond, another big old plane stands at the foot of Richmond Bridge, and beyond a few young trees valiantly soften the northern end of the pompous Richmond Riverside development. Further up, past Asgill House next to the railway bridge, another pair of planes reside, one of which is even taller (reaching over 40 metres) than the Riverside Plane.

51.45645, -0.30386

51.460707, -0.312367

OLD DEER PARK TO SYON PARK

The two riverside planes mark the southern extent of the Old Deer Park, which Richmond Park, or the 'New Park' replaced. It is a much-depleted landscape. The Old Deer Park survives in name, but is now little more than a recreation ground, the larger part of it taken up by the Royal Mid-Surrey Golf Club. The park has gradually changed over the centuries from something that may once have been similar to Richmond Park with all its natural interest and ecological importance, through a Capability Brown landscape in the eighteenth century to the more municipal green patchwork of today. But, whether private or public, all the green spaces in London are part of the same urban forest and contribute to the benefits it bestows on the city. So, while this patch may not be as interesting as some, it is, at least, green.

This corner of south-west London is an area of large and diverse open spaces, often with royal or aristocratic connections. Many of them link together to form a significant natural swathe that runs from Bushy Park to Putney Heath and Barnes Common. Their existence continues to break up the urban areas into distinct communities, and while public access is not universal, much can be explored. A glance at a map or looking out of an aeroplane coming into land at Heathrow shows just how much green space there is around here. This includes a surprising concentration of golf courses, including those at Richmond Park, Hampton Court, Coombe Hill and others. Studies have shown that concentrations of greenery and wealth within cities overlap, seemingly proving that, given a choice, many of us would choose to live surrounded by nature. It's hardly surprising that this is a sought-after part of town.

Our riverside path continues around the loop in the Thames past the Old Deer Park and the large expanse of the Royal Mid-Surrey Golf Club. There is much to see on this less urban, unmanicured stretch. On the landward side, the path is separated by a water-filled ditch, part of the river's flood defences, which conveniently acts as a physical barrier to the golf course and Kew Gardens further downriver. Surrounding the path, a jumble of scrub made up of the usual suspects – bramble, buddleia, sallow, ivy, sycamore, hawthorn, elder, elm and ash – is joined by water-loving willows, poplars and occasional alders. The remnants of very old horse chestnut trees also stand at regular intervals; most are entirely lifeless and all are limbless, but hopeful young twigs sprout from a few. Their upper branches have been removed – presumably for public safety – and their remaining torsos are slowly rotting away, no doubt hosting a cornucopia of insects and fungi.

Part of the river here is unembanked, so it is up to the trees to provide structure. White and crack willows rise to the challenge, and can be seen here in their natural state. They are short-lived, fragile and prone to disintegrate. Crack willow is particularly aptly named. As these bankside trees age, gravity and countless tides cause them to topple into the river, with the current easing their hulks against the bank. Horizontal branches soon push out new shoots and roots, attaching themselves wherever they can gain purchase above the high-tide line.

Surprisingly perhaps, these are joined by self-sown London planes, a species that is commonly planted but rarely seen jumping ship. It seems west London riverside locations represent its idea of home, but they are merely exhibiting characteristics inherited from their original Eurasian parent. That parent, the oriental plane, is associated with watercourses in its native range, so these Thameside trees are simply reverting to type. They're not the giants of parks or avenues, though. Rather, they're opportunistic multi-stemmed bushes – the result of having been frequently cut back or damaged by the river and

51.46448, -0.31943

its debris. Further downstream, around Barnes, there are some larger trees in similar riverside situations, but these are also scrawny. Like the trees in Highbury Fields (p44), they're variable, too. Some have deeply incised leaves, others less so, and their drab bark tends to be rough and fissured, unlike the smooth, flaking grey-and-ochre scales of trees in places such as Kensington Gardens or Green Park. They appear to be the result of cross pollination with different, mostly unnamed, cultivars and perhaps with less common oriental planes, too.

Through a gap in the willows and planes, you can spy uninhabited Isleworth Ait – a momentary vision of a natural riparian wilderness. One of several river islands in the slower waters of the upper Thames, the Ait is managed as a nature reserve by London Wildlife Trust. Access is strictly controlled in order to conserve the rare invertebrates and rich assortment of birdlife found here. Frequently submerged during high tides, it is covered in secondary woodland, which provides ideal cover for thrushes, wagtails and blackcaps, and an excellent vantage point for herons, cormorants and the occasional kingfisher. Some trees on the Ait must have been planted: rocket-like Lombardy poplars, which you can spot rising above the canopy, are always male clones, for instance. Others, such as willows and sycamore, reflect the species found all along this stretch of river and may have arrived unaided. These upper reaches host some of London's elusive native black poplars, too, and the Ait represents what could be an ideal habitat, although they don't appear to be present – yet. 'Invasive' Himalayan balsam, on the other hand, does put in an appearance both on the Ait and on the path where the ground has been disturbed. Like giant hogweed, it is a conspicuous herb and is frequently seen along urban waterways. It is easily identified by its pink, orchid-like flowers that are much appreciated by honey bees in summer. But here on the tidal Thames, it does not appear aggressively invasive, merely eager for a toehold, and it may well find itself outcompeted by larger woody plants shading it out.

Not far beyond the Ait and picturesque Isleworth on the Middlesex bank lies Syon Park. Fronting a largely intact Capability Brown parkscape, unique tidal meadows are submerged by the high tide twice a day. A row of trees – poplars, willows, an alder or two – fix the bank as best they can. Perhaps a native black poplar is also among them but, if so, the unmistakable silhouette of these singularly unkempt

51.46825, -0.32065

51.47304, -0.31462

giants is not obvious. There's a languid sense of natural and historic continuity here, another factor that makes this part of the world so seductive. This is further emphasised as castellated Syon House, sitting timelessly in its remarkable landscape, appears.

On the landward side, as the path approaches the border between the golf course and Kew Gardens, stand some unlikely young trees with large frond-like foliage: North American black walnuts. Some are large enough to bear fruit: clumps of three round nuts, larger than English walnut, give the species away in late summer and autumn. There are dozens here and, a little further on, a large old tree on the land beyond the ditch appears to be their origin. It's difficult to ascertain whether it stands in the grounds of the golf course or in Kew Gardens. Continuing along the towpath, a Turkey oak, a vigorous tree distinguishable from other oaks by its hairy acorn cups, or cupules, comes into view. This species seeds itself readily in London and the path is now roughly level with Kew's oak collection, which contains dozens of different species from all temperate corners of the world. Could the black walnuts and Turkey oak have leapt the fence and be slowly advancing along the riverbank?

KEW GARDENS TO KEW GREEN

The Royal Botanic Gardens, Kew is something of a Garden of Eden – a place where learning and beauty seamlessly combine. It is at once a tourist attraction, scientific institution, and one of the finest arboreta in the world. Kew has also been intrinsically linked to globalisation and British imperialism since its inception.

The gardens originate from around 1759 when Princess Augusta established a garden for 'all the plants known on Earth'. Augusta was the mother of 'mad' King George III, who in later life would spend periods recovering from mental illness at Kew Palace. When George ascended to the throne a year after the gardens were established, the Enlightenment impulse to catalogue and classify natural phenomena was in full swing. Under the guidance of gentleman botanist and Captain Cook's fellow traveller, Joseph Banks, Kew started to build its unrivalled plant collections and expand into a scientific institution. In this new age of exploration and discovery Augusta's original plan must have begun to seem like an endless task.

Later, as the British Empire expanded during the nineteenth century, Kew and its international network became increasingly important for identifying and exploiting the opportunities that newly discovered plant species offered. During this time cinchona from the Andes, source of antimalarial quinine; mahogany from Honduras, and rubber from Brazil were all collected, often surreptitiously, in order to be grown commercially on tropical estates throughout the British Empire.

While it was at the heart of imperial ambitions in the nineteenth century, today Kew is focused on scientific research. Perhaps its highest-profile endeavour is the Millennium Seed Bank Partnership to store seeds from around the world. If Princess Augusta's original mission for Kew seemed ambitious when only a fraction of the world's plants were known, this is a Herculean task that will require decades of commitment. Work started in 1996 and by 2020 it is hoped that 25 per cent of the world's plant seeds will be in storage. The seed bank is like an insurance policy: if any of the plants in its collection should one day become extinct, it might, in theory, serve to re-establish them.

One of Kew's most intriguing attractions has been here, restored, but essentially unchanged, since 1882. It is a small Victorian art gallery near the southern wall that houses the landscape and botanical paintings of Marianne North. Hundreds of her works cover its walls in the nineteenth-century overload style: six or seven deep and hanging so close to each other that their frames almost touch. They represent the plants and natural landscapes that North encountered during the many years she spent travelling, often alone, to places as far flung as Australia, India, Jamaica, Japan and Brazil. Her artistic intention was to capture colourful likenesses of plants and the environments they inhabited, a task that early black-and-white photography and dried herbarium samples were not up to. Unsurprisingly, she was also a distinguished botanist with several tropical plants named after her. The most famous of them is probably Miss North's pitcher-plant, *Nepenthes northiana*, a striking carnivorous species from tropical Borneo. North was also something of an early environmentalist. Recording her concerns about the destruction of old-growth redwood forests by uncontrolled logging in California, she wrote, 'it broke one's heart to think of man, the great civiliser, wasting treasure'.

51.47476, -0.29246

North was at the vanguard of a change in attitude to the natural world. At a time when resources seemed unlimited and ripe for humans to plunder, she began to question the prevailing attitude. While you couldn't exactly characterise her as a tub-thumping eco-warrior, her paintings do at least manage to express the wonder many people have felt for the natural world. North would no doubt agree that plant conservation needs to go hand in hand with conserving the places in which they grow – a concept at the heart of Kew's international work. She would also be disheartened to learn that her handsome pitcher-plant is now vulnerable in the wild. Difficult to propagate, it has been over-collected by commercial plant hunters, while quarrying in the hills where it grows threatens its forest habitat.

The 121 hectares of Kew Gardens are also very much part of the urban forest, not least because of the large number of mature trees and thousands of other plants here. Dating from the time the gardens were established, Kew's five 'Old Lions' still stand: a ginkgo, a pagoda tree, an oriental plane, a false acacia and a Caucasian zelkova – all of them still mere babies compared to the veteran oaks in Richmond Park. Kew's influence on what we grow in the city and beyond has been immense. How many of the familiar plants now found throughout London were first propagated in this corner of the city? The rare trees that have been planted in the last 20 years on the streets and public spaces of Hackney (p92), for instance, are supplied by specialist nurseries, who in turn often take their lead from botanical collections to determine a plant's suitability. Most gardeners and horticulturalists regard Kew's Thameside acres as an extension of their own patches, and many will be quietly monitoring plants in the collection for their aesthetic or commercial suitability. It's also not impossible to imagine, a bit like how rubber tree seeds found their way out of Brazil, that a few seeds or fruits from particularly irresistible plants might occasionally find their way out of the gardens and into private collections…

Leaving Kew by the grand Elizabeth Gate, the spell of picturesque west London remains almost unbroken as the path emerges on to Kew Green. Its Georgian houses and well-kept grassy acreage complete with cricket sight screens are only slightly marred by the South Circular cutting through its eastern side – a reminder that the centre of town is getting closer.

51.48442, -0.29126

BARN ELMS TO BARNES STATION

The river and its <u>adjacent path</u> loops round from Kew Green past
Mortlake before turning off into the interior of the Barnes peninsular.
Barnes, like Hampstead or Blackheath, is one of those London villages
with plenty of green space and attractive houses, many of them adorned
with blue plaques. There's a plethora of restaurants, charming pubs and
chi-chi boutiques, and even a <u>village pond</u>. It sits quietly in a secluded
position between the river and extensive Barnes Common. On its
eastern side, the unprepossessing Barn Elms playing fields adjoin the
London Wetland Centre, a former reservoir complex and now a mecca
for bird spotters.

Between the Wetlands Centre and the playing fields, a scrap of
ivy-cloaked woodland is home to a remarkable survivor: <u>London's oldest
plane tree</u>. It's hard to find, but it is unmistakable once you do. From
a single huge trunk dripping with burrs that gravity has encouraged to
ripple gently downwards, it branches about three metres up into four
trunks, each of them itself the size of a large tree. These branch-trunks
have been chained together and fixed with iron bars. Presumably this
occurred many years ago to keep them from splaying outwards in their
youth – a modern arboriculturist would be appalled by such heavy-
handed intervention. However, it's now too late to save them: the
growing tree has swallowed the metal attachments and with them any
hope of their unchaining. Known as 'Barney', the tree once stood in the
grounds of the long-gone Barn Elms estate, which covered much of the
northern part of the peninsular and was famed for its trees. One early
nineteenth-century account confirms the estate took its name from the
magnificent elms that once grew here. Today there is little trace of them
– just a few scrubby suckers from rootstocks of long-dead trees. Such
suckers are frequent along old railway lines and other places that have
remained undeveloped since the Dutch elm disease epidemic peaked
in the 1970s. Although the dead trees were felled, their extensive root
systems remained below ground, unaffected, and now continue to
throw up hopeful suckers that, in an endlessly cruel cycle, are destined
to succumb to a fresh infection of Dutch elm disease before they reach
maturity. This hybrid plane must have been a curiosity among all the
elms. If, as is thought, it is now around 340 years old, it may well have

been the first of its kind in London and would have been mature in the early nineteenth century – quite probably the largest plane in town.

London planes are a hybrid between two closely related trans-continental species: the oriental plane, *Platanus orientalis*, with deeply incised leaves, and the buttonwood or occidental plane, *Platanus occidentalis*, with much less indented leaves. Like the apple and mulberry, the oriental plane is a tree with an ambiguous native range, originating from the Balkans and east into Asia, possibly as far as northern India. Confusingly, the buttonwood is often known in its native North America as the sycamore, although it is completely unrelated to the familiar London sycamore, a type of maple. The American sycamore grows over much of the continent from Massachusetts to Mexico and crosses the Mississippi into the Midwest. Until Europeans arrived in the Americas, the Eurasian and American species had never met. But then a familiar story unfolded: curious humans could not resist showing off their new finds back home and so seeds of the American sycamore made their way to Europe. No doubt it was soon discovered that it couldn't survive in London's cool summers and mild winters, but the species also arrived in more southerly European latitudes that were much more to its liking. The oriental plane, on the other hand, had been known for centuries in western Europe, including in Britain. John Evelyn knew of specimens in Verulamium (St Albans) and in his 1664 treatise '*Sylva*' speculated that 'they might be propagated to the incredible ornament of the walks and avenues to great-mens houses'.

The oriental and occidental plane are thought to have hybridised in a Spanish or southern French garden in the mid 1600s, resulting in a vigorous tree with characteristics midway between the two parents, most notably in the leaves. So, despite the English name given to the hybrid, the London plane is of continental European origin. Since then, this species, which arose entirely out of human activity, has been rashly planted in boulevards and parks around the world despite us neither knowing exactly how long it can live nor how large it can become.

In the intervening years the pace of global exchange has only increased, and countless more hybridisations, accidental or otherwise, have occurred. Human-enabled mixing of genes is quietly and rapidly – in evolutionary terms – changing species and producing new ones.

And because the greatest diversity of imported species coexists in cities, urban forest are often where these changes happen first. At the same time, other species less able to adapt or which can only live in undisturbed environments are declining at a rate that far outstrips any new arrivals.

From Barn Elms you head to Barnes station, crossing Beverley Brook and passing Barnes Cemetery, a small Victorian burial ground just beyond the tennis courts that marks the southern limit of Barn Elms. The cemetery is overgrown and unfenced, and a modern interpretation board informs you that Richmond council has left it to 'reincorporate' itself into neighbouring Barnes Common, a patchwork of unimproved acid grassland and secondary woodland broken up by roads and the railway: Barnes station is itself on the common. The space is closer in character to old common grazing land than many other expanses of London grassland that have inherited the 'common' denomination – Clapham or Wandsworth, for instance. It is meticulously cared for in order to retain its appearance and conserve the plant and animal communities that live here. The open areas are now mown to stop the trees taking over. In former centuries the land would have been grazed by livestock belonging to local commoners – a wonderful vision that we should surely consider reviving.

Before the station on Queen's Ride, the road passes over the railway line via a humpback bridge and bends slightly to the right with crash barriers appearing on the left. This is where in 1977 a Mini driven by singer Gloria Jones crashed and careered into the trees, tragically killing its passenger, rock star Marc Bolan. A much-visited shrine, more accessible from Gipsy Lane, commemorates the tragedy with plaques and statues to the musician. Masses of plastic toys, decomposing flowers, laminated handwritten fan notes and photographs also adorn the spot. The car's path down the steep roadside bank into the lane below was halted by a sycamore tree, which certainly played a part in transforming the vehicle into a twisted pile of metal. But it may also have stopped it tumbling further and causing more serious injury to Jones, who survived with a few broken bones. Bolan's death was most likely the result of the impact with a metal fence that defined the edge of the road back then; the crash barrier is a more recent innovation. Nevertheless the tree has been blamed for the tragedy. Although badly

51.472836, -0.231176

51.471005, -0.234618

51.467200, -0.241936

51.465912, -0.238562

scarred by the crash, it survived for three more decades, only to be removed some time after 2012 and replaced – somewhat randomly – with a large wooden barrel. For many reasons, sycamores are controversial trees.

VAUXHALL TO KENNINGTON

The train from Barnes passes through a swathe of south London before arriving at Vauxhall where, just around the corner from the station, lies the sanctuary of Bonnington Square. The square and the neighbouring streets of Vauxhall Grove and Langley Lane represent a vision of how an unpromising and once neglected corner of the city can be transformed into a green oasis. Back in the 1970s, the square was compulsorily purchased by Lambeth Council with the intention of building a school. In those days, the city was still in its postwar regeneration phase and, as planned road schemes such as the one at Archway show (p42), authorities were often only too happy to kick people out and bulldoze their homes in the name of progress. At Bonnington Square, the people were moved out, but the houses were not demolished and the school never built. The empty and decaying Victorian buildings were soon squatted and, by the early 1990s, these new residents started thinking about how they could improve their environment.

Walking into Bonnington Square from Harleyford Road, an unusual street tree marking the entrance – a New Zealand long-leaved lacebark – gives a taste of what's to come. Several of the early squatters originated from New Zealand, and the influence of their homeland on the planting is apparent. Further in, a pair of east Asian ginkgoes line the street as it approaches the squatter's original Bonnington Café and, just before the road goes into the square proper, there's a Judas tree. These biblical Mediterranean trees are named after Judas Iscariot who, the story goes, racked with guilt after betraying Christ, hung himself from its branches. As a result the tree's flowers, previously white, blushed with shame and turned magenta. This specific tree is small and seems unsuited to a suicide attempt, but is worth looking out for in May when the pea-like flowers bloom – they can be so profuse that they sprout directly from the branches. Next to it, the Italo café is an ideal spot to soak up the square. Improvements to the pavement have turned it into a kind of mini piazza, complete with beds hosting unusual trees. One of them is planted with an olive tree, partly draped by the wisteria spilling off the front of the café; another is home to a New Zealand lancewood tree. As saplings, these rocket skywards, unbranched and putting out long leathery leaves with toothed edges. With some imagination, their long straight trunks resemble ribboned spears. Even more intriguingly, after 20 years or so, they enter a mature stage, developing a regular tree canopy and rounder, much less remarkable leaves. It is the only tree – on the streets of London at least – with such distinctly different life phases that the juvenile and mature forms could be mistaken for separate species, like caterpillars and moths.

Surveying the square from here, the sheer amount of herbage is striking. Every corner has been planted, and the streets have been narrowed by containers full of yet more plants – a much more attractive traffic-calming measure than humps in the road, but equally effective. It's not just trees: grasses, climbers and old familiars such as hollyhocks and sunflowers embellish every inch of space. The feeling is of a quieter, slower, more friendly place with a strong sense of community, something that's apparent through noticeboards and posters tied to trees. Which came first, the plants or the community? It's hard to say, but it's certain that the greenery has turned the environment into one big, communal garden. The plants must need a lot of maintenance and there's obviously been a lot of planning, both of which no doubt require a strong community focus.

Scooting round the square and the surrounding streets reveal more exotic plants. From New Zealand, there are other types of lacebark and lancewood plus cabbage trees and flax. From other corners of the world, there's a Chinese windmill palm, Italian cypresses and a Mediterranean stone pine – the source of pine nuts – and even a date palm. Elsewhere Indian bean trees, beeches and other big trees of the future are starting to define the canopy under which a whole host of understory species nestles. These include exotic banana plants, a silk tree with pink fluffy flowers in midsummer, a rare Pacific madrone, peanut butter trees and antipodean tree ferns.

To leave the square, take the path through <u>Harleyford Road Community Garden</u>, another twentieth-century glade founded on derelict land. It is much loved and well maintained by volunteers from

Bonnington Square and elsewhere. There must be dozens of similar small gardens, vegetable patches and orchards carved out of formerly unloved corners throughout the city, particularly in more central areas. Such spaces are often established in places or times of decline – immediately after the Second World War, for instance, or when economic or social factors led to depopulation in certain zones. They spring up from dereliction, out of a grassroots impulse to improve the neighbourhood and put abandoned land to good use. Inner city community gardening is thriving and this little haven proves that people are hungry for land to cultivate and nurture.

Heading down the busy Harleyford Road, Kennington Oval cricket ground lies ahead, a bowl covered in creepers and surrounded by well-spaced Lombardy poplars. This unexpected seasonal greenness makes the small sports stadium both stand out and, paradoxically, unobtrusive – an apt reflection, perhaps, of the gentle sport of cricket, so often associated with rural village greens. Following the perimeter of the Oval, the former Cricketers pub, boarded up and gradually crumbling, invites the establishment of a future community garden. It also marks the corner of Clayton Street leading to Kennington Road, one of London's best plane-lined avenues. The old trees here, unlike those on so many streets, are unpollarded and left to reach their full potential. As a result, they are lofty and, when in leaf, provide luxuriant shade from excessive heat and all but the heaviest of summer showers. With fine Georgian houses lining much of the road all the way to the Imperial War Museum, it provides an impressive run-up to central London. The trees on the western side also harbour a secret. Best viewed from the northbound 59 or 159 bus, their trunks have small metal signs attached to them at top-deck height, each bearing the name of an Apollo astronaut, starting with Neil Armstrong outside the Texaco garage. There were once 17, but two – Richard F Gordon and Frank Borman – have been lost, so now only 15 remain. Whether the losses are down to the fact that their trees were felled or the labels removed as lunar-arboreal souvenirs is unclear. The provenance of the metal signs is also unknown. They have been in place since the early 1990s, and their production and fastening was clearly well planned and executed. But why astronauts? Why discrete but long-lasting metal labels? Why attach them to street trees? And why Kennington Road?

Whatever the case, for 30 years they have been a small and subtle intervention that continues to please and puzzle in equal measure. Ultimately, they make this handsome street even more enigmatic.

LAMBETH TO WESTMINSTER HALL

Just before the roundabout at the south side of Lambeth Bridge – resplendent with a group of dawn redwoods – lies the Garden Museum, housed in the former parish church of St Mary-at-Lambeth. The church-yard marks the final resting places of father and son John Tradescant the Elder and the Younger, Lambeth-based gardeners and plant collectors of the 1600s. They had a botanical garden in Lambeth, the former boundary of which is remembered in Tradescant Road between Vauxhall and Stockwell. From there, they introduced many new plants that they brought back from their extensive international travels or exchanged with collectors. The first horse chestnut in London, and for that matter England, was recorded growing there in 1633. John the younger is also often associated with the London plane. It has been suggested that the original hybrid occurred in his Lambeth garden but, given the American parent species' inability to thrive in our mild Atlantic climate, this seems to be an urban forest myth. With more certainty we can say that he introduced numerous species from the British colony of Virginia, including asters, phlox and swamp or bald cypress. Like the dawn redwood, swamp cypresses are deciduous conifers – indeed, it is very hard to tell the two species apart, although the cypress is now much less common. Perhaps this unusual species would have been a more appropriate choice for the Lambeth Bridge roundabout.

On the north side of Lambeth Bridge lies another roundabout, this one with a Canary palm at its centre. With their eye-catching planting, it's almost as if Lambeth and Westminster councils are locked in an inter-borough horticultural battle. Westminster's palm tree has been distinguishing the northern side of the bridge for decades – far longer than Lambeth's fast-growing coniferous upstarts. Little visited, circular and often quite large, roundabouts make ideal spots for planting specimen trees but, like the marooned mini-arboretum at Highbury Corner (p43), their days may be numbered. Cycling groups point to roundabouts' potential for increasing cycling accidents, and urban planners are starting to imagine better junctions and traffic flow designs to benefit all traffic. In this light, the loss of the Lambeth Bridge roundabouts might be a small price to pay for more and safer pedestrian and cycle traffic, which in turn may help hasten the reduction of more polluting vehicles. Heading east from the roundabout towards the Houses of Parliament you pass Victoria Tower Gardens, part of the Victoria Embankment. Beyond Westminster Bridge the scale and ambition of this huge civil engineering project comes into focus: a grand Thames-side boulevard lined with plane trees all the way to Blackfriars Bridge that is mirrored in the Albert Embankment on the south bank.

Before that, though, is the Unesco World Heritage Site of the Palace of Westminster and Westminster Abbey where, at Westminster Hall, this trail ends. Westminster Hall is the oldest part of the Palace. The Norman building dates from 1097, with one significant alteration – the roof, a magnificent oak beam structure that was added at the end of the fourteenth century. It has survived fire, war, weather and redevelopment with just a few nips and tucks to keep it in place since. A marvel of medieval timber engineering, it's the largest hammerbeam roof in northern Europe. Using a complex series of struts and braces to span an area larger than could be covered by single lengths of timber cut from individual large trees, hammerbeam roof technology reached its zenith in the late 1300s. Westminster Hall is vast, and it is worth reflecting on the skill, craftsmanship and labour that must have gone into making and installing the roof so high above the ground with the tools available at the time. It's known that the wood for the roof was assembled and individual vaults fabricated near Farnham in Surrey and then transported by barge to Westminster. The roof's timber, weighing around 660 tons, was the product of hundreds of mature straight-trunked oak trees that were felled from a wide area, including Hampshire, Surrey and Hertfordshire. You might be surprised to learn that the beams were not sourced from woodlands closer to London, such as Epping Forest, Highgate or Lesnes Abbey Wood. But, as they had been for centuries before and were for many years after, these London woods were mainly managed to produce firewood, that most important commodity for cooking and heating in a medieval city. Great builders and shipwrights had to look further afield for their prize timber.

CROYDON
TO
DEPTFORD

NEW ADDINGTON TO HUTCHINSON'S BANK

New Addington is not your average outer London council estate. Beached on a high plateau to the south-east of Croydon, it has one road in, one road out, and since 2000, has been the end of the line of the Croydon Tramlink. The predominantly low-rise estate is notorious to some, unlovely to others, but it is home to 10,000 people. It's also surrounded by greenery, including woods, farms, fields and golf courses. Begun in the 1930s and finished in the late 1960s, its construction was enabled by developers buying up hundreds of hectares of former farmland before postwar planning regulations and the introduction of the green belt effectively ended London's expansion. New Addington's architecture lacks the optimistic brutalism of Roehampton's Alton Estate or the Barbican, but its bucolic position is enviable. There has been some infill, but the street layout has not changed and the surrounding green belt land ensures that – for the time being at least – expansion is kept in check. Unlike more porous city limits in places such as Barnet, here the demarcation between town and country is clear. Cul-de-sacs end in wide tarmacked bays ideal for Ubers and Amazon vans to spin round and beat a hasty retreat once they've picked up or dropped off. Like the human equivalent of a deer park, the estate's houses – terraces, semis and blocks of maisonettes – act like walls imparking it and directing focus to the interior. There's barely a chink in the perimeter but, as those living in the outer housing wall will know, the countryside beyond is quite lovely.

51.34287, -0.01798

Perhaps New Addington's inward-gazing architecture reflects the plateau's political geography. To the north-west, somewhere beyond the farmland lies its estranged, disconnected parent, Croydon. Heathfield, a small Georgian country house that now belongs to the council, is also visible and, rising above the trees on the horizon, a comically branched mobile phone mast failing to masquerade as a pine tree is all too apparent. To the east, sits the borough of Bromley with rolling farmland and downs separating it from the nearest community of Biggin Hill, which, with its Waitrose and gastropubs, is a world away from New Addington. To the west and south lies Surrey – just fields, hedges, woods and villages all the way to the M25 about five miles away.

On the western edge, a steep thorny slope descends into a dry chalk valley: the Hutchinson's Bank nature reserve. It's Croydon all the way to the valley floor where the lowest point marks London's border with Surrey. Like a defensive earthwork, the bank runs for more than half the length of New Addington, though with few gaps between the estate's houses, finding a way on to it from above can be difficult. Nevertheless, a discreet gap exists tucked away on Thorpe Close in the form of an unpromising path leading into the gloom between a fence and a dense hedge. A red Croydon Council sign at the entrance doesn't mention the reserve, instead reading 'The dumping of rubbish or flytipping is strictly PROHIBITED'. Past that, a couple of car wheels, an empty packet of Viagra, some crushed beer cans and a scattering of shiny nitrous oxide capsules garland the transition from urban estate to the countryside. Once beyond, though, the sense of trepidation disappears and the open, unsullied countryside opens out.

Hutchinson's Bank is a patchwork nature reserve of scrubby woodland, dense hedges and a series of small grassy fields, some hosting sheep. At one time, the pasture would have been more extensive, but several grazing-free decades during the last half of the twentieth century allowed the trees to take over. Now the scrub is gradually being cut back to restore the downland that typifies the chalk hills of Kent, Surrey and Sussex. This kind of open grassland is a rare habitat and what exists of it in the world is mostly in southern England. As one of the few parcels of downland on London's southern edge around Bromley, Croydon and Sutton, Hutchinson's Bank is very special. Its poor, dry chalky soils meant the land wasn't used for

51.33677, -0.01393

51.33663, -0.01666

growing crops and Neolithic people cleared it of woodland to graze their livestock – much as the London Wildlife Trust, which now manages the reserve, has been doing in recent years. Over millennia the chalk turf has nurtured specialist interconnected plant and animal communities that are once again returning here.

Late spring, when the wild flowers and butterflies start to appear, is a good time to visit. You need a stealthy demeanour to not only savour the resting butterflies, but also to maximise your chances of stumbling across lizards and slowworms basking in the sun. The sharp-eyed may also spot rabbits in the zone where the grassland and trees meet and, soaring overhead, the sturdy silhouettes of buzzards. Standing still amid downland is supremely rewarding and perhaps the best way to begin comprehending the rich diversity of very small life these seemingly barren slopes support. With few other noises in this patch of London – just a few cars on Featherbed Lane at the bottom of the slope and perhaps a light aircraft taking off at Biggin Hill airfield – it doesn't take long to tune into the quiet cacophony of buzzing and whirring that envelops the place: grasshoppers, crickets, ants, beetles, day-flying moths and thousands of bees are all around.

Dozens of different butterflies can also be spotted – including four types of blue – and parts of the reserve are managed to particularly benefit the small blue. These rare, and disappointingly brown, creatures only feed and lay their eggs on a very limited range of plants, including kidney vetch, which is encouraged here. The kaleidoscope of flapping wings weaving frantically between flowers also includes the pastel blue of common blues, a few bright orange small coppers, multi-coloured peacocks and many others on the brown and white spectrum. The flowers on which they briefly settle belong to diminutive plants that rarely rise more than 30 centimetres above the soil, including bird's-foot trefoil, scabious, marjoram, squinancywort and greater yellow-rattle. Their names have been passed down from a time when dialects of country dwellers who knew and christened them were distinct from harsher city voices. They speak of human co-existence with nature and an intimate knowledge of each plant and its particular characteristics.

Remarkably, in places these plants also include orchids. Yes, barely a hundred metres from New Addington, charismatic common spotted orchids, white helleborines and twayblades can all be found growing wild – not something many London districts can boast. There are a surprising number of native orchids – about 55 – plus dozens of subspecies, varieties and hybrids. Most are unusual, some are very rare, and many are associated with chalk downland. Orchids raise passions, not least among botanists, who are constantly re-categorising and proposing new subspecies or varieties. Getting their name associated with a kind of orchid is the holy grail for many botanists, and orchids oblige by being highly variable, often showing distinct characteristics in specific localities. Although you won't find a 'subsp. *hutchinsonii*' or 'var. *croydonensis*' on Hutchinson's Bank, the common spotted orchids here – just a few miles from Down House where Charles Darwin wrote *On the Origin of Species* and, later, *Fertilisation of Orchids* – may surprise anyone encountering them for the first time. They often appear in clusters, sending up ten-centimetre white-and-pink flower spikes containing numerous individual florets. Look closely and these distinctive orchid flowers reveal themselves: upper petals enclose a bonnet-like structure with a lip-like petal below.

Although orchids may bring to mind large, alluringly exotic blooms – something like the sensual flower paintings of Georgia O'Keeffe – the London versions are small and delicate but nevertheless often exquisite. There's more than a whiff of sexuality about them, too. Orchids look somewhat gender fluid: feminine flowers arise from a pair of underground tubers resembling testicles – indeed '*orchis*' is an Ancient Greek word for testicles. They also flower fleetingly, and much better in some years than others, while their strikingly erect flower spikes stand out in short turf. It's such fickleness, beauty and rarity that make them so enchanting.

FRITH WOOD TO BRAMLEY BANK

A track near to the bottom of the bank becomes Farleigh Dean Crescent, a street of large pre-war detached houses that managed to cut a swathe out of the down before green belt planning regulations were in place. Opposite the end of the road, across Featherbed Lane, a path leads into Frith Wood that marks the boundary between Croydon and Surrey – town and country – with the old oaks of the wood to the left and the immaculately mown fairways of Addington Court Golf Course to the

51.33789, -0.01885

51.34012, -0.02384

right. On a day when golfers are few, the greens become something of a playground for wildlife. Rabbits help keep the turf trim, squirrels lollop across the grass to isolated groups of trees, and pheasants shuffle silently in the distance. Less silent are the ubiquitous chattering London magpies. These green belt birds make every bit as much noise as their inner-city counterparts as they strut around searching for easy pickings.

Frith Wood is dominated by a high canopy of oak trees. These have been left to grow for many decades and show no signs of having been pollarded in the past. As a result, they're big trees with straight trunks, unbranched for ten metres or more, and would make ideal timber for a hammerbeam roof (p120) or palatial half-timbered hunting lodge (p81).

The wood is bounded by another golf course, Farleigh. There are dozens, if not hundreds of courses in these affluent Kent and Surrey borderlands – New Addington and its council houses, it seems, are something of an anomaly. London's green belt was originally conceived to halt the growth of the city and to stop satellite towns from inadvertently joining up to form extended conurbations. In this respect it has proved effective, but as the capital's population continues to grow, can the city continue to accommodate everyone? Politicians seem unable, or unwilling, to deal with knotty planning issues around land use in the green belt, instead allowing London to grow ever upwards and turning a blind eye to activities further out. If we're to keep our green belt, we must also think about the quality of land within it. Publicly accessible swathes of rare downland and ancient woodland are surely preferable to vast acreages of private, manicured golf courses that support far fewer birds, insects and plants.

The chalky path follows the edge of Frith Wood where it takes on a character in between woodland and downland. Chalk-loving whitebeam and wayfaring trees hang over the path along with blackthorn, buckthorn, dogwood and spindle. Whitebeam is associated with chalk more than any other tree: it's almost as if it imbibes so much of the stuff that it seeps out through its leaves. Striking throughout the season, white whitebeam leaves are particularly noticeable in early spring as the buds swell to resemble magnolia flowers, eventually bursting into fresh down-coated oval leaves that shimmer in the April sun.

51.33431, -0.03113

51.33775, -0.03457

Frith Wood comes to an end as 1970s houses appear on the right. This is Forestdale, a large private development built among the trees that's similarly dense to New Addington, but otherwise a different world. Ahead lies Selsdon Wood, a large, mostly ancient woodland where our route joins the London Loop. Like many of the capital's woods, Selsdon has a dense canopy that shades out all but the hardiest of ground flora. It's also home to plants typical of ancient woodland that have co-evolved over millennia and can only thrive in these finely balanced ecosystems. Consequently, many of these 'indicator species' are now rare. Among those found here are the wonderfully named herb paris, a curious, though easily overlooked plant that favours the dankest, darkest corners. A green spike with a whorl of four leaves sends up a single flower that becomes a single black berry, which looks appealingly juicy, but is – be warned – very, very poisonous.

As the wood ends, the path continues through Selsdon's mid-century cul-de-sacs, largely keeping to a track between the houses lined with large field maples, perhaps remnants of a long-disappeared hedge. At Ashen Vale, the path emerges abruptly from its sheltered track to confront the suburbs that until this point have been only glimpses through trees. Across the road, a block of lock-up garages is ineffectively screened by some purple-leaved ornamental plum trees, a staple of 1970s municipal planting. These are younger than that, but may well represent a second or third replanting on the same spot. They flower beautifully in the very early spring, but otherwise have little to recommend them. Known as 'Pissard plum' to horticulturalists, they're often dubbed 'Pissard's purple horror' by those who maintain them.

Crossing Addington Road, the path starts to climb through a narrow tree-lined strip next to a towering metal electricity pylon. Electricity cables are mostly buried among the housing estates of south London, so it's startling to see these large industrial structures here. But at least they're honest, unlike 'disguised' mobile phone masts. Another piece of twentieth-century infrastructure looms through the trees in the shape of the Foxearth Water Tower, a large Germanic concrete affair that also seems out of place in this spot. The path heads right out on to Edgecombe, where another pylon steps through the houses facing the woods, and continues uphill until a track leads into the trees and Bramley Bank nature reserve.

As the ground has risen, the geology has changed. Here the chalk is overlaid with acid sands and gravel that favour different plants. There are patches of common rhododendron, one of London's so-called 'big four' invasive species, along with Japanese knotweed, giant hogweed and Himalayan balsam. But just like those plants, it doesn't exactly seem to have invaded, merely gained a tenuous beachhead – perhaps this is down to effective management.

Bramley Bank is not an ancient woodland, but it does represent what London's posthuman forest might look like if it were allowed back. Big sycamores and pines are interspersed with oak, holly and ash trees, though the sycamore is the one doing all the running, proving what a fine mature tree it can become. Sycamore is hyper-abundant in London. It quickly recolonises rail embankments and other abandoned land. Houses that have undergone a spell of neglect in the past – perhaps because they were rented out as multiple bedsits or left empty when London's population declined in the late twentieth century – now frequently boast large examples in their gardens. Their name refers, puzzlingly, to the 'sycomore', a type of fig with edible fruits found in western Asia and east Africa. Referred to in the Bible, this tree has a broad, shade-giving crown (as many trees do), but that seems to be about the only thing that links it to our tree. The sycamore is a maple and, like all maples, bears its seeds in pairs of winged 'samaras' that helicopter to the ground in autumn. Its Latin name, *Acer pseudoplatanus*, means 'like a plane' and it's true that its lobed leaves are very similar to those of London plane trees. Despite its propensity to grow wherever it can gain a foothold, the sycamore is regarded as non-native on our detached European islands, making it sound like some unwelcome guest whose presence is barely tolerated. But it is a species native to the very near continent, and if sea levels had not risen and cut us off from the mainland after the last ice age, sycamores would no doubt have spread here, too. Perhaps as little as a few more centuries connected to the continent would have been enough for the sycamore to colonise Kent and Essex. Now, though, it's catching up for lost time and its reproductive proficiency is one of the reasons it has lost friends. Gardeners curse its innumerable seedlings and its dense garden-shading canopy (as they also do of lime trees, another source of honeydew), while some ecologists dislike its ability to take root and potentially change the character of ancient woodlands.

Although spoken of as non-native and a species that should be removed, are these terms appropriate? Sycamore plays host to a range of insects, fungi and bird life that find food and shelter in its branches, leaves, flowers and seeds, making it of value to the wider ecosystem. While its pollen is not recorded in post-glacial records, it has been here for many centuries and its introduction may have happened multiple times, both accidentally or aided by humans – its seeds could even have arrived with migrating birds. The point is that sycamores got here one way or another, many years ago, so we should accept them as part of the landscape and rethink the xenophobic labels we have given them. As we don't know exactly when they first took root, perhaps we should just consider them as late arrivals – ones that undoubtedly bring benefits. As well as hosting and feeding other plants and animals, sycamores are handsome trees in maturity with hard, light-coloured timber much admired by furniture makers. But perhaps their strongest card is that they don't have any pathogens lining up to get them, so could make useful replacement trees in the event of an epidemic. This would undoubtedly change the character of the urban landscape, but perhaps that's how we ought to think about evolution.

ADDINGTON HILLS PARK

From Bramley Bank the trail dips downhill through the rhododen-dron-filled gardens of Heathfield House to a vantage point where you can look back to New Addington. Up on its plateau and protected by steep green flanks, it appears like a modern Iron Age hillfort, the population contained, or constrained within – a couple of 1960s tower blocks even give the appearance of lookout towers.

Across Coombe Lane, a path gingerly passes over the tram rails and leads into Addington Hills Park. The geology has changed again here. The dry sandy tracks surrounded by pines give it a vaguely seaside feel and the soil is ideal for acid-loving gorse and heather. Historically, much of this high ground would have been rough grazing, but trees have been allowed to return over the last century or so and Scots pine now dominates. As they mature, pines leave their juvenile conical habits behind and, given enough space, develop characterful broad crowns. Of all the pines, Scots pines, with their orange-tinged bark on higher

51.35698, -0.05699

51.35905, -0.05626

branches, are one of the most distinctive. They do well on these poor sandy soils and given half a chance would dominate the woods up here, so, in the absence of livestock, conservationists work to maintain a balance between woodland and heath. Scots pines are native to northern Scotland, which lies hundreds of miles from London, but that term 'native' means they're regarded differently from the likes of sycamore, even though the latter's native range ends much nearer to the capital.

A broad grassy trail leads through the trees to a viewing platform built in the 1960s to commemorate the 1,000th anniversary of Croydon's founding. Beyond, the high ground suddenly falls away and a steep wooded slope descends below, enabling an unencumbered vista across suburban south London from the rising skyline of Croydon in the west, to the remarkably leafy neighbourhoods that stretch from Selhurst to Sydenham and the pinnacles of Canary Wharf in the distant north-east. Obscuring much of the western city is a long, green ridge punctuated by the twin TV transmitter towers at Upper Norwood and Crystal Palace. The ridge starts around Thornton Heath and extends north-east to Telegraph Hill and New Cross. These northern hills were once covered by the Great North Wood, an extensive area of woodland, commons and heaths that stretched from Selhurst to Deptford, of which now only a few traces can be seen. However, its former extent remains recorded in place names – Norwood, Honor Oak, Forest Hill and Penge, an Old English word meaning 'edge of the wood' – as well as in many other hints on streets and in local features.

As the land below levels off, large twisted oaks similar to those found in the high, heathy part of Lesnes Abbey Wood (p55) appear. These old, tortured trees show past signs of pollarding that has transformed them into curious, ungainly shapes. The woods are bounded by Oaks Road, lined on its north side with generous mid-twentieth century houses partly concealed behind hedges and leafy gardens. More old oaks haphazardly stand along here, long since disconnected from their woodland siblings across the street. They also show signs of pollarding, and at least one multi-trunked tree may have been coppiced in the past. These old characters suggest the woodland might once have stretched further than its current border and that, as with Coldfall Wood (p35), interwar development demanded its reduction.

51.36301, -0.05921

51.36480, -0.05815

51.36531, -0.05973

WEST CROYDON TO THE VICAR'S OAK

Retracing your steps back to Coombe Lane, the tram – more like a suburban train in these parts – takes you through leafy residential Croydon before emerging into the town at Sandilands where it continues along the street to West Croydon. The Overground from here to Anerley passes through the railway junction and marshalling yards at Selhurst. The number of lines that converge here and the space each of them needs to accommodate a 12-carriage train rounding a corner have resulted in a considerable amount of edgeland. Several green islands are marooned among the railway arcs, inaccessible to anyone apart from rail staff and a few very determined graffiti artists. Their vegetation is kept well under control and this landscape of concrete, brick and scrub resembles a kind of post-industrial copse of just two or three years' growth. Unlike ancient coppiced woodland, however, there's a lack of standard trees to provide structure.

Selhurst's self-generated shrubland differs from many secondary woodlands where conservationists have favoured certain plant species over others. This copse is indiscriminately cut and forms an uncurated mass of buddleia, sycamore, bramble and sallow interspersed with holm oak and ash. Other plants are apparent at different times of year: traveller's joy, or old man's beard, with its grey, hairy seeds in winter; mauve Michaelmas daisies in autumn, and bindweed in summer. The list is surely longer, but from the fleeting viewpoint of a suburban train window, it's hard to say just what lives here. No doubt it's a haven for foxes, birds and insects, too.

Heading north up Anerley Road where the street starts to climb, you get a reminder of the former landscape in the guise of Thicket Road, a turning lined with substantial early Victorian houses. Perhaps named after what it replaced, the street bears little sign of a thicket now, but the first house does have a large oak dominating its concreted-over front garden. This old tree may predate the house itself – it's getting on for 200 years – and, when a youthful sapling, could have been hidden in that thorny thicket. Before Anerley existed, this area was part of extensive Penge Common, which once covered a large expanse of the south and east of the Great North Wood complex. Like Barnes Common, Chingford Plain or Bostall Heath, it was once made up of rough grass and heath interspersed with trees and scrub. Anerley was carved out of the common in the nineteenth century, so this tree's provenance as a scrubland hideaway is quite conceivable.

As it climbs, Anerley Road becomes Anerley Hill and views back over the leafy outer suburbs open up behind. At the summit, a road junction appears at the entrance to Crystal Palace Park and, in front of the park gates, a mosaic encircling a tree stump marks the former location of the Vicar's Oak which defined the multiple boundaries that meet here. Today, the boroughs of Croydon, Lambeth, Southwark and Bromley all converge at this spot, but in the past the tree would have marked parish and county boundaries. The oak is long gone and the newly buried stump a stand-in. Why a new tree wasn't planted is a mystery, but John Evelyn recounts in '*Sylva*' what happened to the pair of seventeenth-century adventurers who caused the original's demise – perhaps it's a cautionary tale: '...I am told of the disasters which happened to the two men who (not long since) fell'd a goodly tree, call'd the Vicar's Oak, standing at Nor-Wood (not far from Croydon)... on this oak grew an extraordinary branch of misselto, which in the time of the sacriligious usurpers they were wont to cut and sell to an apothecary of London; and though warn'd of the misfortunes observed to befall those who injured this plant, proceeding not only to cut it quite off, without leaving a sprig remaining, but to demolish and fell the oak it self also: The first soon after lost an eye, and the other brake his leg...'

CRYSTAL PALACE TO SYDENHAM HILL WOODS

Just off Crystal Palace Parade, Farquhar Road marks the site once occupied by the Crystal Palace High-Level railway station. This was the grand terminus of a Victorian line built to bring crowds through the Great North Wood to marvel at the Crystal Palace, which had been relocated from Hyde Park to what was then a corner of Penge Common.

As Farquhar Road curves round, a trio of strange, bulbous street trees appears. They're planes, but quite unlike the great towering trees of the Embankment or Kennington Lane. They all look to be the same age (though what that age could be is anyone's guess) and share much

51.42002, -0.07819

51.42101, -0.07924

in stature and character: large swollen bases to their boles that give way to smooth upper trunks and graceful, rather pendulous branches with deeply cut leaves similar to those of oriental planes. It's thought these squat, baobab-like trees – indeed they're sometimes known as baobab planes – may suffer from a virus that retards their growth and causes this characteristic swelling to occur. There are other examples in the grounds of the Imperial War Museum, Brunswick Square and – home of perhaps the largest and best-known specimen – Ravenscourt Park. But as with other identified plane forms, their origins are puzzling. Their seemingly planned grouping suggests that those who planted them knew of their habits, which possibly debunks the virus theory and indicates they might be a forgotten cultivar.

On the east side of Farquhar Road, past Bowley Lane, the houses give way to Dulwich Upper Wood, a small remnant of the Great North Wood. That this and similar fragments have survived is partly thanks to the long-disused railway, which unintentionally protected the woodland that lined its corridor as south-east London began burgeoning around it. The wood hugs the hillside and lower-lying parts of it were back gardens until wartime bombing destroyed their associated houses and the trees took over. Like the urban wood at Bramley Bank, Dulwich Upper Wood is a mixture of old trees – there are several venerable oaks – and more recent arrivals, including, unsurprisingly, large sycamores. There are also a few remnants from the pre-war back gardens – notably distinctive spotted laurel with its green-and-yellow-speckled leaves, a favourite of Victorian gardeners. Nevertheless, the area is definitely now woodland and through the protection and management of TCV (The Conservation Volunteers), its new character is being encouraged.

Clambering out of the wood on to Crystal Palace Parade, you follow the park round before turning off down High Level Drive, signposted as part of the Green Chain Walk. Named after the railway, the Drive leads into the Hillcrest Estate, a 1960s social housing development built in the hollow between two railway tunnels. Some woodland still intermingles with the estate's tower blocks and maison-ettes, particularly around the tunnel entrances. Here you'll find old oaks, hornbeams and sweet chestnuts, as well as ivy, a plant rarely found in ancient woods. Perhaps its proclivity to entwine itself around more economically important trees made it an unwanted presence, but ivy is

51.42282, -0.07856

51.42644, -0.06956

51.42857, -0.07168

often a significant feature in unmanaged and secondary woods where it happily reclaims the ground that millennia of woodland management have denied it. The great chronicler and interpreter of ancient woodlands, Oliver Rackham, once wrote of a wooded island in an Irish lake – potentially never influenced by humans – where huge ivy trunks 'thicker than a fat man' exist.

Climbing up through the ivy-cloaked woodland surrounding the northern tunnel, the path emerges on Wells Park Road, which itself climbs up to join Sydenham Hill, once the highest point of the Great North Wood. Since the arrival of the railway, Sydenham Hill and its surrounding roads have provided sought-after locations for large houses and generous gardens tucked discreetly among the woods, demonstrating the perennial appeal of urban forest dwelling. On the corner of Crescent Wood Road sits the tastefully greige Dulwich Wood House, once the home of Joseph Paxton, local MP and architect of the Crystal Palace, and now an upmarket gastropub with one of London's nicest beer gardens. Opposite the pub, a white picket fence marks the entrance to steep Low Cross Wood Lane, an ancient woodland track separating Low Cross Coppice, another remnant of the Great North Wood, from Dulwich Wood. At one time, large expanses of woodland such as Epping Forest (p75) were divided into smaller parcels of land with different owners, management cycles and names. It's likely Low Cross Coppice was once a distinct coppice woodland harvested at different times to other neighbouring woods. Now though, Low Cross Wood and Low Cross Coppice are names rarely used. Although preserved in the name of the path, most know the woodland either side as simply 'Dulwich Woods'.

Oak trees from the woods were retained in many of the gardens of the homes built along Crescent Wood Road, which were also embellished with ornamental species, including a few prominent Austrian pines. Number 3 sports a blue plaque in honour of John Logie Baird, one of the inventors of television, and has a delightfully twisted mulberry in its front garden, illustrating how ancient this species can look at a relatively young age – this one is perhaps 150. Across the way, the street's most distinctive building, 'Six Pillars' – a fine 1930s modernist house originally built for a headmaster of Dulwich College – sits under a soaring old remnant oak. Further along, the Dulwich Estate

51.43135, -0.07095

51.43263, -0.07284

51.43315, -0.07247

– an old-established charitable foundation that owns more than 600 hectares of the local area – gave the name of one of its former woods to another sought-after development. Peckarmans Wood is a 1960s-built estate of more modest family houses and perhaps one of London's best-conceived developments of optimistic modern living the woods.

Just beyond Peckarmans Wood lies the entrance to the next woodland tract, Sydenham Hill Wood. Together with Dulwich Woods, it makes up the largest existing part of the Great North Wood and, like Dulwich Upper Wood, has been pieced together from former back gardens, the disused railway and parcels of ancient woodland. Since 1982 it has been managed by London Wildlife Trust, which was instrumental in campaigning to save the wood from developers intent on putting up flats here. An unprecedented number of local residents were galvanised into action and succeeded in halting the building. The community has been deeply involved in caring for and enjoying the wood ever since.

The footpaths running through the wood are well worn. It's clearly a popular place and although not on the same scale as Highgate or Lesnes Abbey Woods, you can still leave the city behind here. You might hear and, if you're lucky, see great spotted woodpeckers; there are nuthatches, treecreepers and sparrowhawks, too. In the summer, early-risers are rewarded with fantastic dawn choruses and in recent years hobbys – small, swift falcons – have bred here, and tiny but striking firecrests have also been seen. At the wood's southern end is a disused and boarded-up tunnel entrance where the line emerged from Hillcrest having driven under Sydenham Hill. It's now a renowned bat roost that's home to common and soprano pipistrelle, common and lesser noctule, and brown long-eared bats.

Sydenham Hill Wood is rich in reminders of its past. On the upper slopes stands a huge cedar of Lebanon that would once have graced a grand back garden, while a Victorian folly reminiscent of a ruined gothic church continues to gently crumble into the wood. Near the cedar lurks a young giant redwood that's too young to be a garden remnant. Maybe, like the redwoods in Hackney's Wick Woodland (p91), it was planted by an urban forester. After all, what would make a better, albeit anonymous, legacy than one of these huge and long-lived trees?

Perhaps the most remarkable thing about the wood is how much nature has returned. Admittedly it had a head start, creeping back from the refugia of the ancient wood fragments that were already here. But within a century the Victorian gardens have become woodland, and after little more than 60 years, the former railway line is barely discernible. Now only the tunnel and Cox's Walk Footbridge are there to remind you of its course. The bridge is the vantage point from which French impressionist Camille Pissarro painted *Lordship Lane Station, Dulwich* in 1871, now in the Courtauld Gallery. What is dense woodland today was open country 150 years ago and the view Pissarro's work depicts is unrecognisable. It looks out north over a rural landscape of patchwork fields as Victorian modernity – in the form of a steam train – hurtles towards you, perfectly capturing the moment when the encroaching city was transforming the countryside around his home in Norwood. Today, of course, it's rather ironic that the view from the footbridge couldn't be more wild, even if that's not true of all its surroundings.

COX'S WALK TO HONOR OAK SPORTS GROUND

Emerging from Sydenham Hill Wood by Cox's Walk – an oak-lined avenue dating from 1732 – comes as something of a shock, spitting you out abruptly on to the car-choked South Circular. But not far away, just before the Horniman Museum, an old oak, surely orphaned from the wood, stands tall on the pavement next to the fuming traffic. It wasn't so long ago that the Great North Wood covered these parts and in the Horniman Gardens more old oaks provide reminders of the past landscape. Following the course of the old railway along the western side of the gardens, on an area managed by the museum since 1972, runs the Horniman Nature Trail – London's oldest nature trail. Beyond Langton Rise, the line disappears to re-emerge at Brenchley Gardens Park where, along the north side, several old trees mark the railway's former route. Among them are a couple of large veteran ash trees that show signs of severe pruning in their past, not unlike how the same species and its frequent embankment cohabitant, sycamore, are treated

51.43827, -0.06684

51.44083, -0.06347

51.44350, -0.06289

today. However, these trees predate the closure of the line in 1954 and perhaps even its 1865 opening.

Roughly halfway along this corridor park, an unruly Persian ironwood tree marks the location of a gate in the perimeter fence and, across the road, the entrance to One Tree Hill. Persian ironwoods are much favoured by municipal parks departments, and many public spaces in London boast at least one. They are smallish trees, with long, gangly upward-sweeping branches sprouting from a low point in their muscular, hornbeam-like trunks. Clothed with oval, beech-like leaves with a distinctive ripple to them, they become head-turning in autumn as they take on dazzling gold, orange, crimson and purple hues. They also reward the curious in February when small, jewel-like red flowers are produced at a time when few other plants are stirring.

One Tree Hill is another Great North Wood remnant and, despite its name, is well-covered in trees. The woodland dates from the 1960s when management of an Edwardian landscaped park that stood here ceased. Back when the park was created in the early twentieth century, London's plane tree craze was in full swing. Dozens were planted here to create a unique patch of plane woodland, though now secondary woodland of ash, sycamore and oak is starting to gain ground. Throughout the urban forest, it's apparent that planes do well as street trees, but not so well in this kind of crowded woodland environment. Many of the specimens here are stunted, some are ailing and a few have succumbed completely. Perhaps they are unable to thrive in competitive, shady woodland and are more at home in the exposed positions that streets, squares and parks offer. The elevated position of the hill is also relatively dry and, as the Thames-side trees in west London show (p108), plane trees appear to flourish by the water.

At the summit, a metal plaque reveals the secret behind One Tree Hill's incongruous name. Situated next to a single low-spreading oak surrounded by railings and a grassy moat, it identifies the tree as the Oak of Honor. Legend has it that on May Day 1602 Queen Elizabeth I rested under the canopy of an oak on this hill after visiting local aristocrat Sir Richard Bulkeley in nearby Lewisham. The current tree was planted in 1905 to replace the original oak honoured by Elizabeth's sojourn and to commemorate the public opening of the hill. In the years leading up to 1905 a protracted battle was fought to keep the hill out of private hands. For centuries locals had been exercising their common rights to access the land. But then in 1896 a fence was erected almost overnight to enclose it. The Enclosure of Honor Oak Hill Protest Committee was formed and a campaign of legal challenges and direct action ensued that lasted nearly ten years. Feelings ran so high that as many as 100,000 outraged locals were motivated to take part in one protest. Eventually, through a series of legal moves, the council was able to compulsorily purchase the land, handsomely paying off a would-be developer from the public purse, and open it for the people in perpetuity.

Just beyond the oak tree, a concrete platform marks the location of a First World War battery where an anti-aircraft gun and its crew were stationed to protect London from the menace of German zeppelin air raids. In front of this, the trees have been cut back just enough to allow visitors to appreciate the commanding view directly north. After the climb up the hill through the woods, the sight of the City framed by branches is worthy of a Hollywood movie: the first awe-inspiring glimpse of a fantastic modern city of glass and steel silently glistening beyond the dense forest.

Descending from One Tree Hill past St Augustine's church, the path emerges on Honor Oak Park where, just before the Overground station, is the entrance to Honor Oak Sports Ground. In the days of Camberwell Borough Council – which was merged into Southwark in 1965 – Honor Oak Nursery occupied land near here. The council-run facility was home to urban plantsmen and the borough 'tree gang', and was where the council's trees, shrubs and flowers were grown before they were planted out in public gardens, parks and streets. Nowadays, increased land values, limited space and reduced council services mean most London boroughs use commercial horticultural businesses to supply the herbage planted in our public spaces. Indeed, well over half of London's trees come from a single nursery, Barcham Trees, in Cambridgeshire. Nevertheless different boroughs still retain distinct local preferences for tree species which have been defined by generations of urban foresters and their sometimes idiosyncratic tastes.

51.45045, -0.05214

51.45005, -0.04949

NUNHEAD CEMETERY TO NEW CROSS GATE CUTTING

51.46032, -0.04884

The approach to Nunhead Cemetery's southern <u>entrance</u> on Limesford Road is, appropriately enough, lined with lime trees. But these are unrulier, smaller trees than the suckering common lime so typical of suburban streets. Nor are they neat small-leaved limes or even glistening silver limes. These Nunhead trees are east Asian Mongolian limes, an unusual slow-growing species now being increasingly planted, and Southwark's urban foresters seem particularly keen on them. They have the heart-shaped leaves common to all limes, but they also have distinctive, coarse teeth that almost obscure their basic cordate outline and in June become laden with fragrant creamy flowers that are magnets for bees.

In the mid-nineteenth century, London was growing rapidly and the graveyards of the city's old parish churches were struggling to accommodate the increasing number of burials as the population boomed. So a series of new cemeteries was established on what were then the edges of the burgeoning city. Collectively, these cemeteries have become known as 'the magnificent seven': West Norwood, Brompton, Kensal Green, Highgate, Abney Park, Tower Hamlets and Nunhead. Nunhead was abandoned in the mid-twentieth century and nature was left to take over. Since the 1980s a dedicated group of volunteers – Friends of Nunhead Cemetery – have been caring for it, including, in places, encouraging the wilderness. At the time of its opening, the cemetery was laid out with tree-lined avenues and individual specimen trees. Today you can still glimpse elderly horse chestnuts through the undergrowth, a lime avenue leading from the northern gate on Linden Grove to the ruined chapel, and a few slowly collapsing but still enormous poplars dotted around.

Turning left on the West Path from the well-kept Limesford Road entrance soon leads into the dark, ivy-smothered eeriness of crumbling angels and foundering memorials. The uncanny sense of this place is heightened by the frequent screeching of ring-necked parakeets zooming through the canopy. At the junction where three of the cemetery's most extravagant tombs are found, the path to the left leads to a <u>viewing point</u>. From here, through a gap in the canopy, you

51.46145, -0.05269

get a clear view of St Paul's, and beyond that, where London's wooded northern slopes start to rise, Nunhead's sister cemetery, Highgate.

Next to the roofless chapel, a numbered post marks the start of the cemetery's Tree Trail. A branch reaching out from the thicket with tell-tale bark patches and distinctive leaves provides a clue to the location of the first tree, a London plane. Those brave enough to venture into the dense thicket will be rewarded with the sight of an enormous burry bole: another baobab plane. This tree is not much taller than the three in Crystal Palace, but the lower trunk must be double the size of theirs – perhaps it was planted soon after the cemetery opened.

Outside the cemetery, Linden Grove, like Limesford Road, is also planted with limes, in this case small-leaved limes. Passing through Nunhead and following the ridge along Kitto Road, the bisected Telegraph Hill Park provides a viewing point west to Denmark Hill and beyond, and north to the City. This ridge above New Cross and Deptford is thought to have been the limit of the Great North Wood, although any sign of it now is long gone. But a bit further along, on Vesta Road, is New Cross Gate Cutting, a rarely open nature reserve and a last vestige of that woodland. Its past is chequered: it once lay on the banks of the Croydon Canal, an early nineteenth-century waterway constructed to take goods from New Cross – where it met the Grand Surrey Canal that connected with the Thames at Rotherhithe – through south London to Croydon. The canal gave way to a railway line, and the land covered by the reserve was used variously to house brickworks and allotments before nature was finally allowed to return. Consequently, this is no ancient woodland, but it does support a maturing canopy, including many Turkey oaks, a tree also much in evidence at Nunhead Cemetery. Turkey oaks originate from south-east Europe and western Asia. They are large and fast growing with less-rounded leaves than native oaks. But their most distinctive feature is bristly acorn cups, resembling, at a pinch, some kind of Ottoman headgear. Turkey oak arrived on these shores in the eighteenth century and has become widely distributed, both through its own efforts as well as those of gardeners and horticulturalists. But through no fault of its own, it's now beginning to fall into the category of 'invasive alien'. The species is one of the two hosts required in the life cycle of knopper gall wasps, which disfigure the acorns of pedunculate oaks. Instead of smooth ovals,

51.46321, -0.05127

51.46736, -0.04641

51.46870, -0.03860

wasp grubs feeding inside the growing acorns create bizarre contorted growths and render them infertile. The following spring a female wasp emerges that lays eggs in the male catkins of Turkey oaks, resulting in a generation of male wasps. And so the triangular relationship continues. In some years, the growing grubs destroy so many acorns that they wipe out a whole generation of oak seedlings before they have the chance to germinate.

NEW CROSS GATE TO SAYES COURT

Jerningham Road is a broad avenue of handsome Victorian houses descending from the once wooded ridge to the floodplain of New Cross and Deptford. The planes that line it were planted either when the houses were built or soon after and, like on so many London streets of a similar vintage, are now kept on a frequent pruning cycle. Usually cut back every three to five years, newly lopped trees take on a harsh blunt appearance that can look particularly callous in winter. This frequent, and expensive, pruning programme is not done to produce a crop of plane withies or even for aesthetic purposes, but to avoid claims against the council for subsidence. The logic is that pruning retards tree growth and so moisture from the soil is extracted at roughly the same level year after year. As soil dries out, it shrinks and cracks, which in turn can cause weak Victorian foundations to shift and buildings to subside. Thirsty trees often get the blame, but if local authorities can show that their street trees are kept under a tight pollarding regime, courts will invariably throw out any claims.

From New Cross Road, you can spot an unlikely tree beginning to tower above the platforms of New Cross Gate station: a youthful giant redwood has launched up out of a sliver of edgeland between the tracks and an empty site. There is no evidence that giant redwoods can produce fertile seed in London, or indeed can germinate here, so it's a mystery how this one arrived. We can only hope that the future developers of the empty plot are enlightened enough to realise the value of retaining and nurturing a growing, giant landmark, which, in its own modest way, it has already become.

Nearby Fordham Park comes as something of a relief after the noise and noxious fumes of New Cross's heavy traffic. From the park's northern edge, on the other side of Sanford Street, a broad pedestrian and cycle route – the quaintly named Woodpecker Road – leads through Deptford's estates and their mature urban landscapes. Underneath the canopy of silver maples and false acacias, this tranquil route shows how estates were imagined in the optimistic mid-twentieth century. Unfussy modernist architecture laid out in leafy cul-de-sacs illustrates a utopian ideal for social housing, but whether life is pleasanter now than in the Victorian terraces they superseded is a difficult question to answer. Certainly, the banning of traffic from Woodpecker Road has made this a pleasant and well-used shortcut, and seems to be a successful model to follow in making other city roads car free.

51.47860, -0.03762

Woodpecker Road ends at Folkestone Gardens, a small urban park created in the 1970s on a Second World War bomb site. Passing under the elevated railway line on to Gosterwood Street takes you through a screen of vigorous poplars. Several species of the genus (including columnar, rocket-like Lombardy poplars) were once frequently planted in London, but, perhaps because they are relatively short-lived and can become very large, are much less so these days. Parallel to Gosterwood Street, Rolt Street leads to Evelyn Street, one of many clues in the local place names that Sayes Court Park is getting closer.

51.48261, -0.03990

Deptford resident John Evelyn (1620–1706) was an aristocratic renaissance man. Instrumental in setting up the Royal Society, the country's first scientific institution, he was a prolific author, diarist and renowned gardener. Of his many books, '*Sylva or A Discourse of Forest-Trees and the Propagation of Timber in His Majesty's Dominions*' is perhaps his best known. It was written to advance knowledge of forestry and trees and to encourage their planting. Evelyn lived – and gardened – for many years at Sayes Court, a riverside estate next to Deptford's naval dockyard. Founded in 1513 by Henry VIII, Deptford Dockyard was where hundreds of the Royal Navy's ships of the line were constructed over several centuries. Evelyn would have been familiar with the workings of the yard and the constant supply of timber needed for shipbuilding, repairs and refits. It has been argued that he wrote '*Sylva*' in part as a response to a Royal Navy request for help securing timber supplies.

51.48491, -0.03122

Now, little remains of Sayes Court and Evelyn's Deptford legacy, save for a few place names and the small Sayes Court Park. The park occupies a fraction of the former extent of the estate, which was famed for its extensive and much-visited gardens. These survived into the late nineteenth century, but now mostly lie buried (along with the historic dockyard) under neighbouring Convoys Wharf, a huge derelict riverside site earmarked for the development of 3,500 homes. But within the park, a remarkable survivor from Evelyn's garden remains in the guise of an ancient, multi-stemmed and extremely gnarled mulberry tree. Like those at Lesnes Abbey and Charlton House, it is surrounded by a fence, and there are several notices to help you interpret it. An ostentatious shiny black boulder with gold lettering and Imperial Eagles supplied by the Russian Embassy says that this arboreal crone was planted in 1698 by Peter the Great. The young tsar had visited Deptford Dockyard to be tutored in the principles of shipbuilding and while there briefly rented Sayes Court from Evelyn. But according to contemporary accounts, the 25-year-old tsar and his raucous chums completely trashed the place – including the famous gardens – so it seems unlikely that he would also have planted a tree during his brief stay. Research carried out on the tree has failed to establish its age, but has shown that it has genetic characteristics of both black and white mulberries, so it could be a hybrid. It's known that Evelyn had both species in his garden, so this could be a relic, or perhaps more likely, a scion from Evelyn's original planting. We know mulberries often look older than they are, and it's easy to see how their fantastic appearances can give rise to equally fantastic tales. As John Evelyn noted in his introduction to '*Sylva*': 'Men seldom plant Trees till they begin to be Wise, that is, till they grow Old, and find by Experience the Prudence and Necessity of it.'

▲

TOWER
BRIDGE
TO
HEATHROW

▼

SHAD THAMES TO THE ALFRED SALTER PLAYGROUND

At the foot of Tower Bridge on Shad Thames, the picturesque cobbled street that runs along the river's south bank, stands a single lofty Lombardy poplar. Tall, narrow trees like these have a relatively small footprint, so fit neatly into tight spots, and their rapid growth makes them attractive to those who want quick results. Named after the northern Italian region of broad fertile plains from which they originate, Lombardy poplars have long been planted en masse to create arboreal screens or windbreaks in flat landscapes. They are a cultivar of the black poplar, but their Italian provenance means they share few characteristics with our own rare subspecies, and, because they are clones of a dioecious tree (one with separate male and female plants), all true Lombardys are male. They have been described, unfavourably, as an 'architect's tree', meaning they look good in visualisations, but are fragile, short-lived and have invasive root systems. Once common London street trees, they are rarely seen around town these days, making the Tower Bridge example something of an anomaly.

In the early twentieth century, the warehouses and industries along the south bank around Tower Bridge found themselves in the borough of Bermondsey, which, like Camberwell (p141), was swallowed up by Southwark as part of a local government reorganisation in 1965. While it lasted, though, Bermondsey council dramatically expanded the urban forest around its factories and docks, from London Bridge to Rotherhithe. In the 1920s and '30s the borough planted nearly 7,000 trees and sowed flowers on practically every parcel of unused land, even developing two special urban-hardy dahlia species, 'Bermondsey Gem' and 'Rotherhithe Gem', for the task. Poplars were among the most numerous trees planted, many of them Lombardys, so the Tower Bridge tree might be regarded as an homage to Bermondsey's pioneering past.

The driving force behind Bermondsey's transformation from industrial slum to green oasis was Ada Salter. A Quaker and ethical socialist, Salter felt her mission was to deal with the great iniquity of slum housing and the intolerable conditions in which the urban poor were forced to live. Originally from Northamptonshire, she had arrived in Bermondsey to work as a social worker, where she met her husband, Dr Alfred Salter. Together they lived in the slums among the people they represented and helped: he provided medical assistance to the poor and needy; she threw herself into alleviating social injustices affecting housing, health, and workers' and women's rights. Salter was elected to the council, and in 1922 became mayor – an important and powerful position back then. She was one of the country's first female mayors, and the first ever woman Labour party mayor. From this platform, she and her fellow councillors set in motion a whole host of radical policies and reforms aimed at improving the lives of the borough's poor. She made great strides in public health decades before the NHS existed; completed a programme of slum clearance and new home building; vastly improved sanitation, and created public washing and laundry facilities. But perhaps Salter's longest-lasting and furthest-reaching achievements came out of the 'Beautification Committee', which she chaired from 1919. This innocuous-sounding task force was driven by Salter's conviction that improving the environment was part and parcel of improving people's lives. She believed that raising citizens' aesthetic appreciation of their neighbourhoods would engender a sense of personal wellbeing and civic pride. Her ambition for the Beautification Committee was to turn Bermondsey into nothing less than a garden city.

Her transformative vision can still be seen throughout the area. Estates dating from the interwar years often have central green courtyards and balconies that, though less festooned today, would once have been bedecked with window boxes. Elsewhere, the legacy of the thousands of trees that were planted is still much in evidence along

Tower Bridge Road, Tooley Street and Jamaica Road – all grand plane-lined thoroughfares. Indeed, virtually every street within the former borough is lined with trees.

Had it not been for the Great Depression of the early 1930s, many more workers' cottages with gardens like those along Wilson Grove and Janeway Street might have been built. Completed in 1928, these developments exemplify the kind of social housing with which Salter wanted to replace the insanitary and overcrowded slums. Rows of neat, faintly art deco garden-cottages were designed in consultation with local women who advised on the practical requirements for their new homes. Greenery was at the heart of the project: gardening was encouraged and the new streets were lined with trees. On Wilson Grove today, large, spreading Caucasian wingnuts cast their shade. These handsome trees with big pinnate leaves (multiple leaflets on a single stem) and long, dangling seed clusters are unusual in London, particularly as street trees, because they require considerable space to reach their impressive potential. These ones may have been planted in 1928 but, more likely, they are replacements for short-lived birches or trees of heaven – the latter was Salter's favourite species. Intriguingly, though, trees of heaven and Caucasian wingnuts have similar leaves and are easily confused, particularly when they are saplings. Perhaps Wilson Grove's wingnuts were planted in error by one of Salter's urban foresters.

Not far from Tower Bridge on Druid Street, opposite the arches carrying the elevated railway lines from London Bridge, is the Alfred Salter Playground. Here, on a raised flowerbed between the swings and the flats of the Fair Street Estate (typical of Bermondsey's low-rise interwar developments), a broad-crowned tree marks the vault where Alfred and Ada Salter's ashes are interred. It's a tree of heaven, between 20 and 30 years old, and one of just a handful deliberately planted in the city in recent years. Salter, though, had cultivated hundreds of them – they were perhaps the species that best defined the work of her Beautification Committee. Originating from China, trees of heaven were introduced to Britain in the 1700s and have been in and out of fashion ever since. Originally regarded as attractive curiosities, they're large trees with huge, almost palm-frond-like leaves and conspicuous reddish seeds that appear in the high canopies in late summer. In the nineteenth century, their pollution tolerance, rapid growth and easy propagation – remarkably, their seedlings and suckers can grow several metres in the first few years – made them good candidates for industrial cities and, by the early twentieth century, they were particularly recommended for planting in the grimier parts of east and south London. After she encountered the species in Paris, Salter was apparently smitten. They appeared to be the perfect tree for Bermondsey, and large examples from her era can still be seen today – Long Lane between Tower Bridge Road and Borough tube station is lined with several fine, mature specimens. But while they are large and fast growing, trees of heaven are also short-lived – they're already in their dotage at 70 – which means the Borough trees might only have a few years left. When their time comes, they'll no doubt be replaced with a different species. Since the mass planting days of the last century, trees of heaven have proven to be invasive, springing up in front gardens, railway embankments, cracks in walls – anywhere they can find a niche. Unlike the misunderstood sycamore, there are many good reasons not to plant them. They barely support other species, they can cause structural damage, poison other plants, and their abundant seeds produce an overpowering or, according to some, appalling smell. In North America they've become known as 'ghetto palms', a reference to their giant leaves and propensity to quickly colonise unused lots. But their past popularity as inner city ornaments mean they're now very much a part of today's urban feral flora. Like buddleia, or giant hogweed before them, trees of heaven appear along the roads, railway lines and waterways that spread out from central London.

THE GUILDHALL TO ST PAUL'S

Across the river to the west of Tower Bridge, the great bulk of the City looms. The oldest part of London, it has been built and rebuilt since the Romans first marked out their outpost of Londinium nearly 2,000 years ago. Except for maybe a couple of centuries after they left, it has been continuously occupied since. Before the Romans, though, there was no settlement here. It's hard to imagine what it must have been like: we know the unembanked, undredged river would have been a wider and less hurried waterway and that, 4,000 to 5,000 years ago, yew trees

were frequent further downstream at Erith and Blackwall. Perhaps
the City would also have been a dense yew wood or, like Epping Forest,
populated by limes. Or maybe alder, willows and black poplar lined the
banks of the Thames and its tributaries, the Fleet and the Walbrook.
Possibly, during the centuries after the Roman withdrawal in around
400AD, woodlands resembling those at Bramley Bank or Nunhead
Cemetery grew up in the pockets of Dark Age wasteland where the
Roman forum, Mithraeum or amphitheatre crumbled.

Turning off Gresham Street, <u>Guildhall Yard</u> opens up into an
Italian-style piazza where Londinium's amphitheatre once stood. You
can see the remains of the theatre several metres below the present-day
pavement in the basement of the Guildhall Art Gallery, on the east side
of the square. The centuries of London detritus – bricks, cement, stone
and bone – that separates the two levels is what passes for soil in the
City and it's surprising anything can grow here. But in the small green
oases that punctuate the streets, trees, in particular, do well. At the west
side of the Guildhall complex, Aldermanbury leads to one of the City's
many green patches, <u>St Mary Aldermanbury Garden</u>. Like other such
spaces in the Square Mile, it sits on the site of a church blitzed beyond
repair during the Second World War and finally laid out as a garden
among the ruins in 1970. Since then it has flourished. Most notable,
perhaps, is an unusual golden-foliaged variety of dawn redwood, while
a pair of large beech trees make it a shady, tranquil spot in high summer.

From here, Love Lane heads west past the Italianate 1960s City
of London Police Station, emerging opposite the tower of <u>St Alban,
Wood Street</u>. This is all that remains of another church that, like St
Mary Aldermanbury, was rebuilt by Sir Christopher Wren after the 1666
Great Fire of London and subsequently destroyed again in the Second
World War. Although lying at the bottom of a human-made canyon of
glass and concrete and surrounded by hard, impermeable pavement, the
tower has trees planted to both its north and south. The northern tree is
a beech, while the southern one is a nettle tree, or European hackberry.
The microclimate on Wood Street is an extreme one – at least by
southern England's mild standards – with the sun's heat magnified by
the reflecting glass and steel during the day, and the stone and concrete
slowly releasing all the daytime heat they've soaked up at night.
Temperatures here will be higher than in the surrounding countryside,

51.51518, -0.09210

51.51637, -0.09305

51.51661, -0.09409

particularly after dark, while winter frosts will be rare. The impermeable canyon floor means that most of the rain runs off into drains rather than filtering through exposed soil to the trees' roots. Life for these two will be difficult: the beech tree has a large flowerbed around it, so that may help, but the nettle tree is out on a limb with just a patch of stone chippings the size of a paving slab to soak up moisture from. Originating from the Mediterranean, urban-hardy nettle trees – so-called because of their nettle-like leaves – are being planted more and more in central London. Able to thrive in the warm and arid conditions of high-rise cities, they and species like them such as olive, crêpe myrtle and mimosa can help moderate temperatures and stave off some of the worst effects of climate change, though many more will be required to make the city more liveable.

Wood Street continues south to Cheapside where, just before the junction, one more of the City's pocket parks lies. St Peter Cheap marks the site of yet another church destroyed in the Great Fire, but one that in this case was not rebuilt. It is now one of the smallest, and one of the oldest, of these green specks. But what it lacks in size, it makes up for in distinction. For who can pass down Cheapside and not notice the towering plane that rises up from here? With a canopy covering an area far larger than the ground from which it springs, the enormous Cheapside plane is one of the Great Trees of London and has been immortalised in countless accounts of the capital. William Wordsworth refers to the location and a singing thrush in his 1797 verse, '*The Reverie of Poor Susan*':

> At the corner of Wood Street, when daylight appears,
> Hangs a Thrush that sings loud, it has sung for three years:
> Poor Susan has passed by the spot, and has heard
> In the silence of morning the song of the Bird.
>
> 'Tis a note of enchantment; what ails her? She sees
> A mountain ascending, a vision of trees;
> Bright volumes of vapour through Lothbury glide,
> And a river flows on through the vale of Cheapside.

51.51440, -0.09483

Surely that song thrush at the corner of Wood Street must have been perched on the bough of a tree? Perhaps one belonging to this noble plane? If so, it must have been a landmark to Wordsworth back then over 200 years ago. The tree's actual age is difficult to judge: though not as huge as the Barn Elms plane (p113), it might be as old. Could it have been planted in the decades after the Great Fire when the City was being rebuilt? It's remarkable to think that the tree has survived in such a busy spot for so long unscathed and, more so, that its presence has halted the development of the buildings in front of it. Just three tiny two-storey shops inhabit this corner of Cheapside – there must be few shorter buildings in the Square Mile.

In step with our growing awareness of the need for more vegetation in the densest parts of the city, street trees have appeared along Cheapside for the first time in recent decades. Walking down here to St Paul's, the vitality of the youthful American sweetgums and Spaeth's alders lining its narrowed roads and widened pavements have turned this once traffic-clogged thoroughfare into a pleasant stroll. Approaching the western end, Wren's great baroque masterpiece comes into view atop the City's highest point. The huge and iconic cathedral survived the Second World War largely intact, a remarkable achievement given so many nearby buildings were completely destroyed or survived only in fragments. The cathedral's surrounding gardens are small but packed with interest. There are familiar London planes, of course, but a number of other more unusual trees emphasise both the surprising fertility of the ground and the mild urban climate. Rising next to a majestic old ginkgo is London's largest giant or grand fir, while against the wall of the south transept, nestling under a huge American sweetgum, stands a rare and rather easily overlooked Japanese bitter orange. This odd shrub is closely related to true citrus trees, but unlike them is deciduous. It also produces oranges, though they're small and apparently very bitter.

St Paul's vast interior is, at first glance, rather more restrained than the exterior. But head to the eastern end and you'll see the baroque style in full evidence in the comparatively intimate wooden choir stalls. Masterfully carved from dark wood with intricate and contrasting tableaux picked out in lighter wood, they're the work of the curiously named Grinling Gibbons, whom many regard as England's greatest woodcarver. Gibbons was living in obscurity in Deptford when, in

51.51444, -0.09599

51.51362, -0.09735

1671, his eminent neighbour John Evelyn, no less, stumbled across him carving by candlelight. Evelyn immediately recognised Gibbons' talent and that same day described what he had seen to his great friend, Christopher Wren. Soon after, Gibbons was commissioned to work on the choir for St Paul's and his tremendous talent flourished.

Gibbons was able to transform oak and lime wood into exquisite forms that belie the lumpen, hard material from which they are carved: garlands of flowers, fruits and leaves and individual heads of *putti* (baroque cherubs) cut from light lime wood and set off against dark oak. The rich patina of this structural oak work, built up over more than three centuries, gives the carved cartouches, panels and architectural forms a solidity that emphasises the lightness of touch in the lime carving. Since the Middle Ages, lime wood has been the material of choice for northern European wood carvers, who valued its relative softness, lack of grain and the ease with which it could be shaped. Although Gibbons worked in London, it's difficult to say where his materials came from. The oak may well have been locally sourced, but the lime wood used for much of the most exquisite work at St Paul's is unlikely to have been harvested in London.

CAREY STREET TO VICTORIA EMBANKMENT

Off Chancery Lane, Carey Street leads you out of the City's boundaries. To the south lie the Victorian-era Royal Courts of Justice and to the north, behind the 1602-built <u>Seven Stars</u> – which has a good claim to being London's oldest pub – is Lincoln's Inn, one of the four Inns of Court to which all barristers belong. The usually quiet Seven Stars is a fine vantage point from which to admire the row of dawn redwoods that subdues the gothic fussiness of the Royal Courts. Maybe the narrowness of the street exaggerates their height, but these must be some of the tallest examples in London, even if they are perhaps only 30 years old.

Serle Street, opposite Carey Street's westernmost tree, leads to <u>Lincoln's Inn Fields</u>, London's largest, and one of its earliest, squares. The space became a model for dozens of other townhouse developments arranged around central, communal green areas that were to be built

51.51489, -0.11349

51.51595, -0.11471

over the next centuries. London's squares became sought-after addresses and are often synonymous with lavish private gardens accessible only to residents. These gardens tend to be old, and as a result have become forest sanctuaries for a wealth of plant and animal life in the heart of the city. Cheapside might now be sadly bereft of the thrushes that Wordsworth immortalised, but bird watchers should have more luck here, less than a mile away, in Lincoln's Inn Fields.

The Fields have a particularly rich and varied history. Originally common land on the edge of the city, they were laid out as a residential square in the first half of the 1600s, although the central open space was not enclosed until the following century. Camden council now maintains it as a public park and, perhaps because of this varied past, it doesn't have the same feel as smaller and younger Georgian squares, such as Brunswick or Bedford, with their spectacular canopies.

Just a block from the relative tranquillity of Lincoln's Inn Fields, Kingsway typifies a later, grander architectural style of broad new thoroughfares befitting a powerful imperial city. This great Edwardian avenue, together with the Aldwych at its southern end, was engineered to allow for regularly spaced soil-filled pits suitable for planting large trees. Perhaps inevitably, those trees were London planes. Most of them are still here today and they have decades, if not centuries, still to go. Now they lean ever further away from the buildings that hem them in – some are considerably less than 90° from the pavement – with the effect that their canopies reach over the road to almost touch.

The Aldwych curves round to meet the Strand, which was presumably once right above the river's high water mark. Certainly, until the completion of the Victoria Embankment 150 years ago, it was much closer to the foreshore of Old Father Thames than it is now. The Embankment project transformed the older, more expansive river into the narrower, faster flowing and walled waterway we know today. Stretching from Blackfriars to Westminster, it enclosed London's new sewer system and created a new broad riverside avenue. As with Kingsway and the Aldwych, trees were an integral part of the vision. For several decades, British travellers had witnessed the construction of magnificent new avenues in Europe's great cities. Haussmann's *grands boulevards* in Paris, with their wide streets of elegant buildings and consistent lines of trees, typified the developments, inspiring

51.51568, -0.11924

51.51154, -0.11907

51.50941, -0.11934

impressionist artists such as Gustave Caillebotte and one-time
Norwood resident, Camille Pissarro (p139). Pissarro's *The Boulevard
Montmartre at Night* in the National Gallery's collection exemplifies the
ways city streets were being transformed in the late 1800s. But it wasn't
until the completion of the Victoria Embankment that London finally
had anything to rival those Parisian boulevards.

Trees were planted along the length of the Embankment on both
sides, in places as double avenues – two trees on each side of the street.
The London plane was chosen for the job, though at the time it was
known simply as the plane or hybrid plane. The species had much to
recommend it: it could tolerate the pollution of the carbon-fuelled city, it
was easy to propagate from cuttings, it grew fast, and it kept its attractive
leaves late into autumn. Such a sensation was the Victoria Embankment
when it opened in 1870 that, within a few years, new tree-lined streets
were being planned and developed across the city. A craze had begun
and the avenue tree, usually the plane, came into its own. With some
notable exceptions, the majority of London's plane trees were planted
after the completion of the Thames Embankments. Few are more than
150 years old and many still stand today. If planes are able to survive the
effects of pathogens lining up to cause problems, they have centuries of
life left in them and future generations of Londoners can look forward
not only to the beauty of their old age, but also to the environmental
benefits these large trees provide in cities.

By the end of the nineteenth century, the planting of trees was
well-established as a prerequisite for any new street with aspirations,
and much could be told about those aspirations by the species chosen.
Writing about Camberwell in his 1961 book *Victorian Suburb*, one urban
historian, Harold Dyos, says: 'The choice of trees, too, had its social
overtone: planes and horse chestnuts for the wide avenues and lofty
mansions of the well-to-do; limes, laburnums and acacias for the middle
incomes; unadorned macadam for the wage-earners.'

Now so familiar, the phenomenon of street tree planting is a
relatively recent innovation. What started as a way to add municipal
grandeur to broad boulevards became a means of distinguishing a
street's social status as London's suburbs grew. In more recent years,
the diversity of species has increased dramatically and the planned,
human-made spread of the urban forest throughout the capital now

covers many of those streets of 'unadorned macadam'. Today there are estimated to be around 900,000 street trees in London, a considerable swathe of the urban forest, and as we learn more about how trees make cities more liveable through the ecosystem services they provide, that number will, we must hope, grow.

OXFORD STREET TO HYDE PARK

From the Embankment, the route heads north up Charing Cross Road and to the junction with Oxford Street, London's busiest shopping thoroughfare. Beyond its treeless eastern half (reflecting the historic correlation that the east has always been less green than the more affluent west), the road widens beyond Oxford Circus and trees start to appear.

Perhaps surprisingly, though, the trees on this most polluted and popular of streets are not planes. Instead, they're rather diminutive and lacklustre Chanticleer pear trees. A cultivar of the Asian callery pear, the Chanticleer pear is much planted in London – some say over-planted – but is easy to overlook. Its neat habit and relatively restricted growth means it is straightforward and cheap to manage, but because it doesn't attain the size of a plane, its pollution-absorbing benefits are correspondingly less. As other pears, Chanticleers flower and, for a few fleeting days in early spring, their blossom can offer unexpected respite to the shoppers pounding the pavement here. But unlike orchard pear trees, they don't produce large, potentially hazardous fruit. Instead scant brown berries develop that even the birds appear to shun. Oxford Street obviously needs tough trees, and while the Chanticleer pear may not be everyone's favourite, it can certainly cope with a lot. A callery pear in New York known as the 'Survivor Tree' miraculously recovered after being pulled from the rubble of the World Trade Center in the wake of the 9/11 attacks, so Oxford Street seems well within its comfort zone. But shouldn't this most iconic of London streets be planted with a more charismatic species? Paris's main shopping street, the Boulevard Haussmann, for instance, is lined with planes – perhaps they would also make Oxford Street grander and, in the longer term, greener.

Just by Bond Street tube station, Davies Street leads to Berkeley Square in the heart of Mayfair. Like Lincoln's Inn Fields, it has seen many changes since it was created in the mid-eighteenth century

51.51429, -0.14914

and lacks architectural consistency, with only a few original buildings surviving. Large and rectangular with an <u>oval garden</u> at its heart, it's surrounded by roads busy with taxis and supercars and only a pair of zebra crossings enables access. Despite its shortcomings, though, it is also home to some of central London's oldest trees. The magnificent towering planes that dot the gardens have been here since 1789 and one of them has been designated a Great Tree of London. In truth they are all worthy of the accolade and any visitor would be hard-pressed to know which of the 20 or so holds the title. All are in remarkably good shape for trees that have survived in such a busy place for so long. There are signs they may have been pollarded at horse-head height in their distant past, which has resulted in swollen lower trunks and a few trees developing two or three branched trunks above the historic pollard line.

As well as being some of London's oldest urban trees, they are also some of its most valuable – incredibly, the Great Tree of London here is worth £750,000. The amount reflects not the tree's timber, but its 'community value'. The Capital Asset Value for Amenity Trees (CAVAT) is a framework that was devised, for those who require such base analogies, to put a price on a tree. Created by the London Tree Officers Association – a trade body representing those who manage the urban forest – CAVAT values are derived through a complex formula that takes into account how big a tree is; how many people it benefits by cleaning the air, moderating temperatures and so on; and how long it can be expected to live. CAVAT valuations can be called in if, say, a developer constructing a new apartment block decides it needs to fell a row of street trees in order to complete the job. The idea is that a builder faced with a charge potentially running into millions would decide against cutting down century-old plane trees merely to place a crane or create access for a bulldozer. However, some worry that putting a finite value on a tree might simply encourage developers to factor the cost of tree removal into their budgets. On the other hand, while thinking of trees as assets with values may not chime with our more romantic notions of nature, it does arguably follow in the footsteps of the woodsmen who once made their livings from them.

<u>Hyde Park Corner</u> marks Mayfair's south-western extremity, beyond which the Royal Parks of Hyde Park and Kensington Gardens lie. Originally a deer park like Richmond, Hyde Park became a public

space in the 1600s and, together with adjacent Kensington Gardens, makes up the largest open space in central London. Wandering around you can almost cut out the surrounding city. Traffic noise lessens the deeper you venture, though the numerous towers rising above the canopy around the perimeter are rather harder to screen off. In truth Hyde Park is probably not the place to come for a simulation of the countryside. This is very much a human-made landscape with a considerable amount of social, royal and national history attached to it. Instead, it might be better regarded as a clearing in the urban forest, a kind of managed wood pasture where humans and other city-dwelling lifeforms gather. Those human gatherings take many forms: the park is certainly a place of sanctuary where people can relax and breath more easily. In the past the aristocracy met here and it has also hosted military encampments. In more recent times, though, it has become best known as a site of protest and of new ideas. As well as the location of Speakers' Corner on its north-eastern edge, Hyde Park was once home to the Reformers' Tree, where in 1866 protestors gathered to urge lawmakers to give all adult men the vote. Its position is now marked by a mosaic. Then, at the beginning of the twentieth century, suffragettes held the 'Women's Sunday' rally here with the aim of persuading the government to give women the vote. At the time, it was the largest demonstration ever held in Britain.

Hyde Park was also, of course, the site of the Great Exhibition in 1851. Its Crystal Palace, which would be relocated to Penge three years later (p135), stood on the southern side of the park and was so vast that it could accommodate two large pre-existing elm trees inside its vaulted glass structure. Hyde Park and Kensington Gardens were once both famous for their elms, which were planted during the early 1700s in avenues that criss-crossed the parks. The avenues are still there but the elms, many of which survived into the twentieth century, have all since succumbed to Dutch elm disease. They were replaced by limes and planes, many of which, particularly the planes, have reached magnificent proportions. There are also fine examples of large silver limes, and hundreds of other species grow here too. In recent years the park has been managed to encourage wildlife: grass has been left unmown and reed beds have been allowed to develop around parts of the lake. As a result, many birds and insects now make

51.51092, -0.15877   51.50908, -0.16139

51.50284, -0.16913

their homes here, too. One of the most evident is the Egyptian goose, several of which can usually be seen around the Serpentine lake. Small for geese, but certainly not ducks, these glamorous African birds with distinctive dark circles around their golden eyes exist in growing feral populations around several London lakes. Elsewhere, you might hear the chatter of reed and sedge warblers, you'll almost certainly see and hear ring-necked parakeets, and if you're lucky, you could even spot the odd bird of prey: sparrowhawks breed here, kestrels hover and little owls occasionally perch on higher branches.

SLOANE SQUARE TO MARGARETTA TERRACE

The lower reaches of Sloane Street have been planted with Turkish hazel trees, a species now much in favour among urban tree planters. Unlike our native hazel bushes, these become large, conical single-trunked trees with grey, corky bark. But in other respects they are similar, producing conspicuous male catkins in very early spring, while their rounded leaves are only differentiated by their more ragged edge. Turkish hazels are most easily identified by their nuts, which in autumn can become very apparent. The strange spiky clusters can often be found discarded on pavements below the trees, while above, squirrels feast on their contents.

Before Sloane Square, a quiet turning on the left, Wilbraham Place, has been planted with a range of unusual trees, some of which are so rare that this might be one of the few places to see them. Like the mini arboretum at Highbury Corner, the local authority appears to be trying out new species that might one day adorn more streets in Kensington and Chelsea. First, there's a handkerchief tree, which features dramatic white blooms resembling small pieces of hanging cloth, and – beyond a relatively common variegated tree privet – a Catalina ironwood. This strange evergreen tree with peeling red bark is only found on a few small islands off the coast of southern California – the Channel Islands – but it is doing well here, even if it is a little unruly to pass muster on all but the most bohemian of streets. Further along, there's another surprising rarity, a chinaberry or Persian lilac from south-east Asia. An altogether more elegant tree than the ironwood, it has a tendency to throw out doubly pinnate leaves with leaflets along multiple secondary stalks, like those of the Kentucky coffeetree, and produces discrete blue flowers in late spring. Both the Catalina ironwood and the chinaberry come from latitudes much more southerly than our own, so it must be the warming climate, or the urban heat island effect, or both that makes London mild enough – particularly in winter – for them to thrive.

Heading south beyond Sloane Square, you reach the venerable Chelsea Physic Garden on Swan Walk. Founded in 1673, this one-and -a-half hectare slice of the urban forest has an especially mild micro-climate that allows tender plants to flourish, including a regularly fruiting grapefruit tree. The nearby River Thames moderates the fiercest winter chill and combines with the urban heat island effect to create a temperate enclave. Pre-dating the Royal Botanic Gardens at Kew by nearly a century, the Physic Garden was established by the Worshipful Society of Apothecaries to provide herbs for London's medical trade and carry out research. And as global trade and exploration burgeoned in the seventeenth and eighteenth centuries, it also found itself at the centre of an international network of plant exchange. The garden's history is intricately tied up with that of Irish physician Sir Hans Sloane, who is remembered in several place names around Chelsea and by a statue in the garden. Sloane was an apprentice here before qualifying as a physician and sailing off to the Caribbean, where he collected many new and exotic plants. While in Jamaica, he also advantageously married Elizabeth Langley Rose, an heiress to slave-holding sugar plantations. On his return to London, Sloane continued to add to his extensive collection of flora, fauna and other curiosities which, on his death, he passed to the nation. The objects would form a significant part of the British Museum's founding collection, while his natural history artefacts are now housed at the Natural History Museum. Among those are his original herbarium samples, which include his original cocoa plant specimen. Sloane is credited with introducing the recipe for sweetened chocolate mixed with milk to England, which quickly became a popular hot drink and, with some refinements, a product on which future fortunes would be built.

Today the Chelsea Physic Garden feels like a not-very-well-kept secret. It's a delightfully intimate and manicured place full of fascinating plants, but one you will probably need to share with many others if you visit. A nineteenth-century painting shows a couple of handsome cedars of Lebanon shading the garden which are, alas, no more. Unlike at Kew, where the five 'Old Lions' – heritage trees – remain from its opening (p112), no plants survive from the garden's early years. Today, a large old (perhaps a century or more) olive tree with multiple trunks might be regarded as the senior plant. At one time, olive trees were unusual in London and thought to be tender. Now, though, they're a frequent sight and thrive in the urban environment. Whether this is a sign of the changing climate or simply their increased availability is hard to say. Either way, their blanket planting in fashionable front gardens seems to show the species' perceived tenderness may not be an issue in twenty-first century London.

From the Chelsea Physic Garden, it's not far along the plane-lined Chelsea Embankment to the Albert Bridge where Oakley Street heads north. Completed in 1850, this, plus nearby Margaretta Terrace and Phene Street, were the very first London thoroughfares to have trees systematically planted in their pavements. Sadly, those original trees are now long gone, save, perhaps, for a single towering plane with ivy covering its lower trunk halfway up Margaretta Terrace.

SOUTH KENSINGTON TO GUNNERSBURY TRIANGLE

Heading further north towards South Kensington tube station across Fulham Road, you reach Sydney Place, a fine stuccoed London terrace typical of the affluent streets of Kensington and Chelsea. Unusually, though, this relatively narrow street is home to a row of half a dozen dawn redwoods that serve to emphasise its architectural consistency. On the paved piazza at the tube station, more perpendicular trees sprout from the pavement, although like the Lombardy poplar at Tower Bridge, these are a broadleaf species. They're cypress oaks, fastigiate cultivars (with branches sweeping upwards) of the pedunculate oak, which add a regimented structure to the space, while also helping cut out some of the relentless traffic fumes on this busy corner.

From South Ken, the District Line rattles west, occasionally breaking the surface until it emerges definitively above ground after Hammersmith. From here, the elevated line passes right over Ravenscourt Park, bisecting it into a small southern parklet and a main northern expanse, which is home to two Great Trees of London. In a playing field fenced in as a playground, one of them competes with a pair of flanking planes. It's a particularly soaring tree of heaven which, like the similarly towering trees in Bermondsey – those on Long Lane (p154) near Borough tube station, for instance – must now be in its dotage. The other Great Tree here is even more special, a baobab plane, perhaps the biggest, and most likely the fattest, example in the urban forest. Like those at Crystal Palace (p136) or Nunhead Cemetery (p143), it has the characteristic squat, pot-bellied trunk from which a mass of low-spreading branches emerge. But it is altogether bigger. Much bigger. From a distance, it looks like a large, ancient oak similar in shape to the Royal Oak of Richmond Park (p104). But its car-sized bole isn't hollow, suggesting that it's more youthful. The tree is such a landmark that a local myth has sprung up about how it came to be. The story goes that it was once a lofty plane like others in the park, until it took a direct hit from a Second World War bomb. What you see today is the partly recovered, blasted wartime stump. Apocryphal as it is, the tale expresses something of what we feel about trees: standing solidly rooted to the spot, they survive against all the odds, particularly in the city, miraculously putting out new leaves every spring in a constant cycle of renewal and regrowth.

Beyond Ravenscourt Park, largely treeless King Street becomes plane-lined Chiswick High Road, marking the borough boundary between Hammersmith and Fulham, and Hounslow. Leafy residential streets lead off to north and south, though the turning into Chiswick Lane is marked by an unusual street-side conifer in a walled, raised flowerbed. It is a low and spreading blue-tinged Atlas cedar from Morocco, marking what seems to have been a forked junction, one prong of which is now paved over. Conifers are rarely seen as street trees, perhaps because they're perceived to be too shady, but as this Chiswick cedar shows, they can be distinctive landmarks. What's more, by photosynthesising all year long, they can go on oxygenating the city

51.496876, -0.236698

51.496693, -0.236698

51.49275, -0.25173

in winter when deciduous trees are dormant. Is it nothing more than arboreal fashion that holds back urban foresters from planting more firs, pines, cedars and spruces?

At Acton Lane the path heads north to the entrance of Gunnersbury Triangle on Bollo Lane, just across the road from Chiswick Park tube station. The nature reserve was created accidentally by three intersecting railway lines. Just west of Turnham Green station, the District Line splits into two broad arcs that a bit further ahead are in turn crossed by the Gunnersbury-South Acton Overground line. Together the three tracks trace an equilateral triangle of squeezed, convex sides to create a patch of railway-bounded, disconnected edgeland similar to the island at Selhurst junction (p134). Over the years, the enclosed two-and-a-half hectares were put to various uses, from gravel extraction to allotments, before nature was allowed to return after the Second World War. In the early 1980s plans to develop the site were met by local protests, eventually leading to a public inquiry that ruled the land should be managed for wildlife conservation. This landmark decision marked the first time an inquiry found in favour of protecting urban nature. Since the mid-1980s, the Triangle has been managed by London Wildlife Trust on behalf of Hounslow council and is now a remarkable environment of secondary natural habitats – mostly woodland with several ponds and a meadow towards the north-west tip. It supports a huge diversity of plants and animals and, if you're lucky, you might spot a red-crested green woodpecker slowly slinking through the grass as it feeds on ants. Bulkier, shier and a more muted green than the lime-green parakeets that screech constantly overhead, green woodpeckers can be seen in quiet clearings throughout the city.

Gregarious ring-necked parakeets on the other hand, are highly visible all over London, but seem to particularly favour the west. Hundreds of them gather at night to roost in nearby Wormwood Scrubs from where they fan out across the city each morning. They are easy to spot as they zoom, screaming through the sky in dazzling green flocks before descending on food plants. These birds are not fussy eaters and can strip the fruit or seeds off anything from a grape vine to a hornbeam. They have been making occasional appearances in London since the nineteenth century, the result of captive birds escaping – or being released – into the wild. Breeding was first recorded in Kent back in 1969 and since then, numbers have grown rapidly, particularly in the last 30 years or so. They originate from subtropical India but, despite our weather, appear quite happy in London. It's not known exactly how they arrived, but several urban legends have evolved to explain their presence. Of these, the two most repeated are either that they escaped from the set of 1951's *The African Queen* at Isleworth Studios, or that Jimi Hendrix released a pair in Carnaby Street in the 1960s. Neither story stands up to much scrutiny, but the birds must have come from somewhere, and in the space of a few decades, they've adapted brilliantly to life in the urban forest. The RSPB estimates there are around 8,600 pairs in the UK, with the largest concentration in London. The British population represents one of the northernmost outpost for parrots anywhere in the world and they have become one of London's most iconic birds, perhaps second only to the feral pigeon.

HOUNSLOW TO HEATHROW

At the end of Bollo Lane, the Piccadilly Line from Acton Town jolts its way west towards Heathrow and, like the Central Line in Essex, enters open country between Boston Manor and Osterley, crossing a large swathe of park and farmland, plus an inevitable golf course. This is the Brent river valley and Osterley Park, which together represent one of the largest open spaces in west London. But, as the sight of urban Hounslow soon confirms, the greenery is a temporary respite.

51.50294, -0.28069

Leaving Hounslow West station, it's a short walk south to Hounslow Heath, the last 80-hectare remnant of what was once a vast heathland stretching from Hounslow in the east to Staines in the west, and north, through Heathrow, to Harlington. Originally a royal forest, by the thirteenth century it was common land used largely for grazing, suggesting it was a patchwork of open grassland and heaths interspersed with small pockets of woodland. The current landscape reflects these historic uses: grazing cattle still keep the scrub at bay and a large central area has returned to a heathland of gorse, broom and heather. Signs at the entrances warn walkers to keep their dogs on leads and to watch out for adders. The only venomous snake found in the UK, adders are very rare in London, and Hounslow Heath represents one of only four sites where they still cling on.

51.46285, -0.38800

This scrubby patch is therefore very important, and not just for adders. Around 350 types of moth have been recorded here – a huge number. Although a few moth species are doing well, a large majority are in sharp decline across the capital. Attractive Jersey tigers are abundant in summer, but its relative the garden tiger, once very common, has virtually disappeared. New arrivals such as box tree moths, whose caterpillars exfoliate box hedges; oak processionary and horse chestnut leaf miner moths are all conspicuous, too. But what about the dusky thorn, the grizzled skipper, the shoulder-striped wainscot, the rosy rustic or the dot moth among many others? The dusky thorn has declined by 98 per cent in 30 years and others also continue to disappear. No doubt our activities are affecting their survival: the destruction of specialist habitats, intensive farming practices outside the capital, and the problems our increasingly brightly lit city causes for night-flying moths may all be part of the problem. A downturn in moth numbers matters because an ecosystem that has less diversity is bad for all the life within it, making it easier for pests and diseases to take hold and for the web of subtle and complex dependencies to break down. If moths are in decline, other voiceless life will be, too.

On the western side of the heath, nearly covered by the under-growth, a large sign, partly covered by bindweed and brambles, reminds us that this was once a golf course with its own special rules about stray golf balls. It states: 'Any ball crossing the line of the white posts at any time is out of bounds, regardless of where it lands.'

These days the golfers and white posts are long gone and just this esoteric sign and a few unlikely trees – Lombardy poplars and cypresses – provide clues that this might be London's only abandoned golf course. Previously owned and managed by the local authority, Hounslow Heath Golf Club shut its doors in 2016 due to poor attendance and rising costs. Its reclamation by the heath may be short lived, however, with plans afoot to reopen a new course. But if the heath's inexorable return can help bring the adders back, perhaps it might also galvanise urban nature lovers to ask questions of the local community about whether another golf course really is the best use of this land. Who knows, in ten years' time, Hounslow Heath may be larger than it is today.

This corner of Hounslow undoubtedly offers cause for hope, but there's no escaping it's also a noisy spot. The roar of jet engines

51.4595, -0.3967

is constant as hundreds of planes a day thunder above the treeline to land at Heathrow a couple of miles to the north-west. Traffic also hums in the distance, picking up speed on the motorways and expressways that abound, while construction noises add more discordant tones, with the heavy clanking of concrete and metal accompanied by the rhythmic warning beeps of reversing or unloading vehicles. But at least on the Heath and in the Crane valley, the din is partially blocked and the vegetation filters out the worst of the traffic emissions.

From Hounslow Heath, the route follows the River Crane upstream towards the airport. This sparkling brook once flowed through the vast heath along a wooded corridor where herons perched far more frequently than they do today. While pollution has caused a decline in the number of fish, the woodland ribbon offers sanctuary to many birds and insects. Across the Staines Road, the path enters Donkey Wood where a boardwalk meanders through wet woodland dominated by impressive alders and, to a lesser degree, largely Dutch elm disease-resistant wych elms. The next road that crosses the Crane is Causeway, and a short section of the valley wood stretches beyond to the busy A30, which marks the southern boundary of Heathrow Airport.

The river and its wooded valley nevertheless continue and, indeed, broaden to create a natural buffer against the airport. Along the grim Eastern Perimeter Road the divide between Heathrow and the Crane valley is stark. The trees provide an effective boundary, quietly muffling the diabolical airport from the residential streets of Cranford. We often call upon nature to separate one land use from another, or to shield us from places we would rather not see or hear. In this sense we seek to contain nature, but we should remember that it will ceaselessly seek to expand its territory. The Crane Valley park might be regarded as a wildlife refuge, from where plants and animals might one day recolonise the lost heathland that for now lies buried beneath the concrete aprons, runways and terminals of Heathrow. Beyond the perimeter fence, fluorescent-suited humans in white hard hats wield strimmers, drive grass mowers and deploy bird-scaring devices as they toil to keep the latent urban forest in check.

While the airport itself is practically denuded of all but human activity, it's also a point of arrival for grains of life from far-off places. How many of us have wittingly or unwittingly brought home plant or insect life – in clothing, on a beach towel, on the sole of a shoe, maybe – from our travels around the world? We've all heard about scorpions or tarantulas arriving with fruit consignments from the tropics, and no doubt Heathrow airport has greeted many of these unexpected visitors. As we travel in increasing numbers to an ever greater variety of destinations, and demand an ever wider selection of foods and plants, our airports will be where new species make their bridgeheads.

Arriving by bus in the geographical heart of the airport between Terminals 2 and 3, some half-hearted landscaping has been carried out to soften the worst excesses of this nightmarish complex of buildings and roads. In the anti-pedestrian environment around Heathrow Central bus station, it's just possible to walk for a hundred metres or so. Rows of manicured hedging plants are interspersed with sorry-looking trees – including a few cabbage trees from New Zealand vainly trying to anticipate the palm-fringed oases in which lucky passengers might soon find themselves landing. In some clipped Norway maples a small flock of starlings provides welcome confirmation that at least a few birds have managed to successfully negotiate the incessant traffic, barren concrete and perilous flight paths to arrive in this grey, human-made island.

But perhaps the most heart-warming sight is that of a self-sown sapling clinging on to the roof of a non-descript brick building in the shadow of a high-rise car park. This tenacious little tree is a silver birch, a pioneer species that thrives on heathland. It's certain to be one of the first to recolonise as soon as its time comes.

51.47137, -0.45339

51.471265, -0.454137

SPECIES

The following is a list of specific species mentioned in the book.
It contains flora, fauna and fungi; it does not contain genera
(for instance 'sunflower' or 'poplar') that often have multiple species
associated with them. It is ordered alphabetically by scientific name.

FLORA (TREES)

Abies grandis	Giant or grand fir
Acacia dealbata	Mimosa or silver wattle
Acer campestre	Field maple
Acer davidii	Père David's maple
Acer negundo 'Flamingo'	'Flamingo' variegated box elder
Acer platanoides	Norway maple
Acer pseudoplatanus	Sycamore
Acer saccharinum	Silver maple
Aesculus hippocastanum	Horse chestnut
Ailanthus altissima	Tree of heaven
Albizia julibrissin	Silk tree
Alnus glutinosa	Alder
Alnus × spaethii	Spaeth's alder
Arbutus menziesii	Pacific madrone
Betula papyrifera	Paper birch
Betula pendula	Silver birch
Betula utilis var. *jacquemontii*	Himalayan birch
Callistemon laevis	Bottlebrush tree
Carpinus betulus	Hornbeam
Carpinus betulus 'Fastigiata'	Fastigiate hornbeam

Carya ovata	Shagbark hickory
Castanea dentata	American chestnut
Castanea mollissima	Chinese chestnut
Castanea sativa	Sweet chestnut
Catalpa bignonioides	Indian bean tree or southern catalpa
Catalpa speciosa	Western catalpa
Cedrus atlantica 'Glauca'	Atlas cedar
Cedrus libani	Cedar of lebanon
Celtis australis	Nettle tree or European hackberry
Cercis siliquastrum	Judas tree
Chilopsis linearis	Desert willow
× Chitalpa tashkentensis	
Citrus × paradisi	Grapefruit
Clerodendron trichotomum	Peanut butter tree or glorybower
Cordyline australis	Cabbage tree
Cornus sanguinea	Dogwood
Corylus avellana	Hazel
Corylus colurna	Turkish hazel
Crataegus laevigata	Woodland or midland hawthorn
Crataegus mollis	Scarlet thorn
Crataegus monogyna	Common hawthorn
Crataegus phaenopyrum	Washington thorn
Crataegus punctata	Spotted thorn
Cupressus sempervirens	Italian cypress
Davidia involucrata	Handkerchief tree
Euonymus europaeus	Spindle
Fagus sylvatica	Beech
Fagus sylvatica 'Cristata'	Cockscomb beech
Fagus sylvatica 'Purpurea'	Copper beech
Ficus carica	Fig
Fraxinus excelsior	Ash
Ginkgo biloba	Ginkgo
Gleditsia tricanthos	Honey locust
Gymnocladus diocica	Kentucky coffeetree
Hevea brasliensis	Rubber
Hibiscus syriacus	Hibiscus
Hoheria sexstylosa	Long-leaved lacebark
Ilex aquifolium	Holly
Juglans nigra	Black walnut
Juglans regia	English walnut

Koelreuteria paniculata	Golden rain tree or pride of India
Lagerstroemia indica	Crêpe myrtle
Ligustrum lucidum 'Excelsum Superbum'	Variegated Chinese tree privet
Liquidambar acalycina	Chang's sweetgum
Liquidambar styraciflua	American sweetgum
Lyonothamnus floribundus	Catalina ironwood
Malus domestica	Apple
Malus sylvestris	Wild crabapple
Melia azedarach	Chinaberry or Persian lilac
Metasequoia glyptostroboides	Dawn redwood
Metasequoia glyptostroboides 'Gold Rush'	Golden dawn redwood
Morus alba	White mulberry
Morus nigra	Black mulberry
Olea europaea	Olive
Ostrya carpinifolia	Hop hornbeam
Parrotia persica	Persian ironwood
Paulownia tomentosa	Foxglove or princess tree
Phoenix canariensis	Canary palm
Phoenix dactylifera	Date palm
Pinus nigra	Austrian or black pine
Pinus pinea	Stone pine
Pinus sylvestris	Scots pine
Platanus occidentalis	American sycamore or occidental plane
Platanus orientalis	Oriental plane
Platanus × hispanica, or Platanus × acerifolia	London plane
Poncirus trifoliata	Japanese bitter orange
Populus alba	White poplar
Populus nigra subsp. *betulifolia*	Black poplar
Populus nigra 'Italica'	Lombardy poplar
Populus tremula	Aspen
Prunus cerasifera	Cherry plum
Prunus cerasifera 'Pissardii'	Pissard plum
Prunus spinosa	Blackthorn
Pseudopanax crassifolius	Lancewood
Pterocarya fraxinifolia	Caucasian wingnut
Pyrus calleryana 'Chanticleer'	Chanticleer pear
Pyrus pyrifolia	Nashi or sand pear
Quercus cerris	Turkey oak
Quercus ilex	Holm oak
Quercus petraea	Sessile oak

Quercus robur	English or pedunculate oak
Quercus robur 'Fastigiata'	Cypress oak
Quercus suber	Cork oak
Quercus × hispanica 'Lucombeana'	Lucombe oak
Rhamnus cathartica	Buckthorn
Robinia pseudoacacia	False acacia
Robinia pseudoacacia 'Frisia'	Golden false acacia
Salix alba	White willow
Salix caprea	Sallow or pussy willow
Salix fragilis	Crack willow
Sambucus nigra	Elder
Sequoiadendron giganteum	Giant redwood
Sorbus aria	Whitebeam
Sorbus aucuparia	Rowan or mountain ash
Sorbus domestica	True service tree
Sorbus torminalis	Wild service tree
Styphnolobium japonicum	Pagoda tree
Syringa reticulata	Japanese lilac
Taxodium distichum	Swamp or bald cypress
Taxus baccata	Yew
Taxus baccata 'Fastigiata'	Irish yew
Tetradium daniellii	Bee-bee tree or euodia
Tilia cordata	Small-leaved lime
Tilia mongolica	Mongolian lime
Tilia tomentosa	Silver lime
Tilia × europaea	Common lime
Trachycarpus fortunei	Chinese windmill, or Chusan palm
Ulmus americana	American elm
Ulmus glabra	Wych elm
Ulmus procera	English elm
Viburnum lantana	Wayfaring tree
Viburnum opulus	Guelder rose
Zelkova carpinifolia	Caucasian zelkova

FLORA (OTHER SPECIES)

Anemone nemorosa	Wood anemone
Anthriscus sylvestris	Cow parsley
Anthyllis vulneraria	Kidney vetch
Asperula cynanchica	Squinancywort
Aster amellus	Michaelmas daisy
Aucuba japonica	Spotted laurel
Buddleja davidii	Buddleia
Calluna vulgaris	Heather
Calystegia sepium	Bindweed
Cephalanthera damasonium	White helleborine
Chamaenerion angustifolium	Rosebay willowherb
Clematis vitalba	Traveller's joy or old man's beard
Cryphonectria parasitica	Sweet chestnut blight
Dactylorhiza fuchsii	Common spotted orchid
Fallopia baldschuanica	Russian vine
Fallopia japonica	Japanese knotweed
Fistulina hepatica	Beefsteak fungus
Hedera helix	Ivy
Heracleum mantegazzianum	Giant hogweed
Impatient glandulifera	Himalayan balsam
Laetiporus sulphureus	Chicken of the woods
Lotus corniculatus	Bird's-foot trefoil
Neottia ovata	Twayblade
Ophiostoma novo-ulmi	Dutch elm disease
Origanum vulgare	Marjoram
Paris quadrifolia	Herb paris
Phormium tenax	New Zealand flax
Pteridium aquilinum	Bracken
Rhinanthus angustifolius	Greater yellow-rattle
Rhododendron ponticum	Common rhododendron
Rubus fruticosus	Bramble
Scabiosa columbaria	Scabious
Theobroma cacao	Cocoa
Ulex europaeus	Gorse

FAUNA (BIRDS)

Accipiter nisus	Sparrowhawk
Acrocephalus schoenobaenus	Sedge warbler
Acrocephalus scirpaceus	Reed warbler
Alcedo atthis	Kingfisher
Alopochen aegyptiaca	Egyptian goose
Ardea cinerea	Grey heron
Athene noctua	Little owl
Buteo buteo	Buzzard
Certhia familiaris	Treecreeper
Columba livia	Feral pigeon
Dendrocopos major	Great spotted woodpecker
Egretta garzetta	Little egret
Erithacus rubecula	Robin
Falco subbuteo	Hobby
Falco tinnunculus	Kestrel
Garrulus glandarius	Jay
Motacilla alba	Pied wagtail
Motacilla cinerea	Grey wagtail
Motacilla flava	Yellow wagtail
Phalacrocorax carbo	Cormorant
Phasianus colchicus	Pheasant
Pica pica	Magpie
Picus viridis	Green woodpecker
Psittacula krameri	Ring-necked parakeet
Regulus ignicapillus	Firecrest
Regulus regulus	Goldcrest
Sitta europaea	Nuthatch
Sturnus vulgaris	Starling
Sylvia atricapilla	Blackcap
Sylvia undata	Dartford warbler
Troglodytes troglodytes	Wren

FAUNA (INVERTEBRATES)

Aglais io	Peacock butterfly
Andricus quercuscalicis	Knopper gall wasp
Apis mellifera	Honey bee
Arctia caja	Garden tiger moth
Chameraria ohridella	Horse chestnut leaf miner moth
Cupido minimus	Small blue butterfly
Ennomos fuscantaria	Dusky thorn moth
Euplagia quadripunctaria	Jersey tiger moth
Hydraecia micacea	Rosy rustic moth
Leucania comma	Shoulder-striped wainscot moth
Lucanus cervus	Stag beetle
Lycaena phlaeas	Small copper butterfly
Melanchra persicariae	Dot moth
Neozephyrus quercus	Purple hairstreak butterfly
Pararge aegeria	Speckled wood butterfly
Polygonia c-album	Comma butterfly
Polyommatus icarus	Common blue butterfly
Pyrgus malvae	Grizzled skipper moth
Thaumetopoea processionea	Oak processionary moth

FAUNA (OTHER ANIMALS)

Anguis fragilis	Slowworm
Capreolus capreolus	Roe deer
Cervus elaphus	Red deer
Dama dama	Fallow deer
Homo sapiens	Human
Lacerta vivipara	Lizard
Muntiacus reevesi	Muntjac
Nyctalus leisleri	Lesser noctule bat
Nyctalus noctula	Common noctule bat
Oryctolagus cuniculus	Rabbit
Pipistrellus pipistrellus	Common pipistrelle bat
Pipistrellus pygmaeus	Soprano pipistrelle bat
Plecotus auritus	Brown long-eared bat
Sciurus carolinensis	Grey squirrel
Vulpes vulpes	Fox

FURTHER READING

BASFORD, KATHLEEN, The green man (Paperback edition). *Woodbridge: D. S. Brewer, 1998*

BURTON, RODNEY M., Flora of the London area (First edition). *London: London Natural History Society, 1983*

COOPER, FIONA, The black poplar: Ecology, history and conservation (First edition). *Bollington: Windgather Press, 2006*

CROSBY, ALFRED W., Ecological imperialism: The biological expansion of Europe, 900–1900 (Second edition). *Cambridge: Cambridge University Press, 2004*

DARRELL-LAMBERT, DAVID, Birdwatching London: All the best places to see birds in the capital (First edition). *London: Safe Haven Books, 2018*

DYOS, H., Victorian suburb: A study of the growth of Camberwell. *Leicester: Leicester University Press, 1966*

ELLIOT, PAUL A., British urban trees: A social and cultural history, c. 1800–1914 (First edition), *Winwick: The Whitehorse Press, 2016*

EVELYN, JOHN, Sylva: Or a discourse of forest trees, volumes 1 and 2 (Reprint of the fourth edition). *London: Forgotten Books, 2015*

FARJON, ALJOS, Ancient oaks in the English landscape (First edition). *Kew: The Royal Botanic Gardens, Kew, 2017*

FIENNES, PETER, Oak and ash and thorn: The ancient woods and new forests of Britain (First edition). *London: Oneworld Publications, 2017*

FITTER, R. S. R., London's natural history, volume 3 in the New Naturalist series (First edition). *London: Collins, 1945*

FOLEY, MICHAEL AND CLARKE, SIDNEY, Orchids of the British Isles (First edition). *Cheltenham: Griffin Press Publishing, 2005*

GILBERT, BOB, The green London way: Walking the city's history and wildlife (New edition). *London: Lawrence and Wishart, 2012*

GIROUARD, MARK, The English town (First edition).
London: Yale University Press, 1990

GRINDROD, JOHN, Outskirts: Living life on the edge of the green belt
(First edition). *London: Sceptre, 2017*

GOODE, DAVID, Nature in towns and cities, volume 127 in the New
Naturalist series (First edition). *London: William Collins, 2014*

HOSKINS, W. G., The making of the English landscape (Reprint of the first
edition). *London: Penguin, 1985*

JOHNSON, OWEN AND MORE, DAVID, Collins tree guide: The most complete
field guide to the trees of Britain and Europe (First edition). *London: Collins, 2004*

JOHNSTON, MARK, Street trees in Britain: A history (First edition).
Oxford: Oxbow Books, 2017

JOHNSTON, MARK, Trees in towns and cities: A history of British urban
arboriculture (First edition). *Oxford: Oxbow Books, 2015*

JONNES, JILL, Urban forests: A natural history of trees and people
in the American cityscape (First edition). *New York: Viking, 2016*

LAKE, SOPHIE; LILEY, DURWYN; STILL, ROBERT AND SWASH, ANDY, Britain's
habitats: A guide to the wildlife habitats of Britain and Ireland (First edition).
Woodstock: Princeton University Press, 2015

LANDRETH, JENNY, The great trees of London (First edition),
London: Time Out Guides, 2010

MABEY, RICHARD, The unofficial countryside, introduced by Iain Sinclair
(First edition). *Wimborne Minster: Little Toller Books, 2010*

MACCARTHY, FIONA, William Morris (Paperback edition).
London: Faber and Faber, 1995

MANLEY, CHRIS, British moths and butterflies: A photographic guide
(First edition). *London: A & C Black Publishers, 2008*

MCDOWELL, DAVID, Richmond Park: The walker's guide
(Revised and enlarged edition). *London: David McDowell, 2006*

PEARCE, FRED, The new wild: Why invasive species will be nature's
salvation (First edition). *London, Icon Books, 2015*

RACKHAM, OLIVER, Ancient woodland: Its history, vegetation and uses
in England (New edition). *Dalbeatie: Castlepoint Press, 2003*

RACKHAM, OLIVER, The history of the countryside: The classic history of
Britain's landscape, flora and fauna (Paperback edition). *London: Phoenix, 1997*

RACKHAM, OLIVER, Trees and woodland in the British landscape:
The complete history of Britain's trees, woods and hedgerows (First revised
paperback edition). *London: J.M. Dent, 1993*

RILEY, GLENDA, Women and nature: Saving the "wild" west (First edition). *Lincoln: University of Nebraska Press, 1999*

ROGERS, KENTON; SACRE, KEITH; GOODENOUGH, JESSICA AND DOICK, KIERON, Valuing London's urban forest: results of the London i-tree eco project (First edition). *London: Treeconomics London, 2015*

SOLMAN, DAVID, Loddiges of Hackney: the largest hothouse in the world (First edition). *London: The Hackney Society, 1995*

STACE, CLIVE A. AND CRAWLEY, MICHAEL J., Alien plants, volume 129 in the New Naturalist series (First edition). *London: William Collins, 2015*

STAFFORD, FIONA, The long, long life of trees (Paperback edition). *London: Yale University Press, 2017*

TABOR, RAY, A guide to coppicing (First edition). *Bath: Eco-logic Books, 2013*

TAYLOR, GRAHAM, Ada Salter: Pioneer of ethical socialism (First edition). *London: Lawrence and Wishart, 2016*

WEBSTER, A. D., London trees. *London: Swarthmore Press, 1920*

WILLIAMSON, TOM; BARNES GERRY AND PILLATT, TOBY, Trees in England: Management and disease since 1600 (First edition). *Hatfield: University of Hertfordshire Press, 2017*

USEFUL WEBSITES

Ancient Tree Forum: *ancienttreeforum.co.uk*
Conservation Volunteers: *tcv.org.uk/london*
Friends of Nunhead Cemetery: *fonc.org.uk*
London i-Tree Eco Project: *forestry.gov.uk/london-itree*
London Tree Officers CAVAT: *ltoa.org.uk/resources/cavat*
London Wildlife Trust: *wildlondon.org.uk*
London's Mulberry Tree Heritage: *moruslondinium.org*
Plane Trees in London: *aranya.co.uk/planes*
Royal Botanic Gardens, Kew: *kew.org*
Royal Parks: *royalparks.org.uk*
RSPB: *rspb.org.uk*
Tree Musketeers: *sustainablehackney.org.uk/tm*
Trees For Cities: *treesforcities.org*
TreeTalk – London Street Tree Map: *treetalk.co.uk*
Woodland Trust Ancient Tree Inventory: *ati.woodlandtrust.org.uk*

INDEX

ACKNOWLEDGEMENTS

I would like to thank the following people who have given me the benefit of their knowledge and advice during the process of writing this book: Rupert Bentley Walls, Peter Coles, Graham Coster, Mathew Frith, Andrew Stuck and especially Katherine Pogson for her support, love and invaluable fine-tuning.

Intriguing snippets, fortuitous introductions and very useful suggestions came in many forms and from many people including Scott Barkwith, Valerie Beirne, Simon Edwards, Peter Fiennes, Bettina Metcalfe, Stephen Middleton, Xanthe Mosley, Sadie Palmer, Steve Pocock, Jefferson Smith, Graham Taylor and Carole Wright.

I'd also like to thank the team at Quadrille, particularly commissioning editor Zena Alkayat for her ongoing encouragement, and Nick Funnell for his diligent and thoughtful editing. As well as Nikki Ellis, Robin Howie, Céline Hughes and Claire Rochford. And finally, thank you to all those people on social media who share my passion for trees, nature and London, and have been the source of much valuable information.

A FEW TREES
OF NOTE

A. Golden Rain Tree, *The Charterhouse*
B. Beech Pollard, *Epping Forest*
C. Horse Chestnut, *Walthamstow*
D. Chang's Sweetgum, *Hackney*
E. Mulberry, *Lesnes Abbey*
F. Field Maple, *Frank's Park*
G. Caucasian Wingnut, *Wilson Grove*
H. Cockscomb Beech, *Greenwich Park*
I. Mulberry, *Sayes Court*
J. Giant Redwood, *New Cross Gate*
K. Sycamore, *Bramley Bank*
L. Grapefruit Tree, *Chelsea Physic Garden*
M. Catalina Ironwood, *Chelsea*
N. Royal Oak, *Richmond Park*
O. 'Barney', *Barnes*
P. Riverside Plane, *Richmond*
Q. Pagoda Tree, *Kew Gardens*
R. 'Baobab' Plane, *Ravenscourt Park*
S. The Totteridge Yew, *Totteridge*
T. Hornbeam, *Coldfall Wood*